Lesbian Configurations

BETWEEN MEN ~ BETWEEN WOMEN
LESBIAN AND GAY STUDIES

LILLIAN FADERMAN AND LARRY GROSS, EDITORS

Advisory Board of Editors
Claudia Card
Terry Castle
John D'Emilio
Esther Newton
Anne Peplau
Eugene Rice
Kendall Thomas
Jeffrey Weeks

Between Men ~ Between Women is a forum for current lesbian and gay scholarship in the humanities and social sciences. The series includes both books that rest within specific traditional disciplines and are substantially about gay men, bisexuals, or lesbians and books that are interdisciplinary in ways that reveal new insights into gay, bisexual, or lesbian experience, transform traditional disciplinary methods in consequence of the perspectives that experience provides, or begin to establish lesbian and gay studies as a freestanding inquiry. Established to contribute to an increased understanding of lesbians, bisexuals, and gay men, the series also aims to provide through that understanding a wider comprehension of culture in general.

Lesbian Configurations

renée c. hoogland

Columbia University Press
New York

Columbia University Press
Publishers Since 1893
New York   Chichester, West Sussex
Copyright © 1997 renée c. hoogland

First published in 1997 by Polity Press in association with
Blackwell Publishers Ltd.

Library of Congress Cataloging-in-Publication Data

hoogland, renée c., 1960–
     Lesbian configurations / renée c. hoogland.
        p.   cm. — (Between men ~ between women)
     Includes bibliographical references and index.
     ISBN 0–231–10906–7 (cloth) — ISBN 0–231–10907–5 (pbk.)
     1. Lesbianism in literature.   2. Lesbians in literature.
3. Lesbianism in motion pictures.   I. Title.   II. Series.
PN56.L45H66   1997
809'.93353—DC20   96–38895

♾
Casebound editions of Columbia University Press books are
printed on permanent and durable acid-free paper.

Printed in Great Britain by Hartnolls Ltd, Bodmin, Cornwall

c 10 9 8 7 6 5 4 3 2 1
p 10 9 8 7 6 5 4 3 2 1

Contents

Acknowledgements

This book was as much born from excitement as indignation: excitement about the growing visibility of lesbian sexuality in Western cultural production, and indignation about the particular settings, or configurations, in which mainstream 'lesbian' images consistently (re)appear and, more often than not, subsequently disappear. Such a combination of irritation and fascination has always been an 'enabling' state of mind for the kind of work in cultural analysis I am interested in. In this case, my ambivalence about recent lesbian configurations got me started on a project that, although I had not been consciously aware of it, had begun to take shape during innumerable conversations with friends, colleagues and students in preceding years. I am grateful to all these various interlocutors who, each in their own ways, have helped me to see what this book eventually should be. Needless to say, responsibility for the views expressed in the chapters that follow rests solely with me.

Impossible as it may be to trace my ideas to their 'rightful' origins, there are a number of people whose contributions to their development I wish explicitly to acknowledge. I thank my friends and colleagues Marijke Rudnik-Smalbraak, Dorelies Kraakman and Jan Willem Duyvendak for their unfailing willingness, both now and in the past, to discuss many of the vexing questions that continue to inform my work. I further owe a special debt to Maaike Meijer and Judith Roof, who both read the entire manuscript at its different stages, and whose invaluable comments not only did much to improve the final result, but also, on occasion, forced me seriously to reconsider what I had thought I wanted to say.

The Centre for Women's Studies at the University of Nijmegen generously allowed me a leave of absence in which to complete the manuscript. The Netherlands Organization for Scientific Research provided me with a grant that made it possible to spend a semester at the Institute for Research on Women and Gender at Stanford University. I am grateful to the Staff and Affiliated Scholars at the IRWG, who rendered my sabbatical leave not just a much-needed period of uninterrupted work, but also one of genuine inspiration. I especially wish to thank my fellow Visiting Scholars Ellen Peel and Stephanie McCurry for their practical and material support, as much as for their friendship and stimulating conversation.

I thank my editor, John Thompson, for soliciting this book, and for his unabating faith in the project while it was under way. I also wish to acknowledge the press's two anonymous readers who helped me to tighten up parts of my argument, and to clarify some of its underlying ideas.

I dedicate this book with love to Pamela Pattynama, to whom I owe more than I can say.

A short section of chapter 1 appeared in 'Heterosexual Screening: Lesbian Studies', in *Women's Studies and Culture: A Feminist Introduction to the Humanities*, ed. Rosemarie Buikema and Anneke Smelik (London & New Jersey: Zed Books, 1995). Chapter 3 grew out of an essay published in *Modern Fiction Studies* 41.3 (1995) under the title 'Hard to Swallow: Indigestible Narratives of Lesbian Sexuality'. Chapter 4 first saw the light in *The Journal of Narrative and Life History* as '(Sub)textual Configurations: Sexual Ambivalences in Sylvia Plath's *The Bell Jar*', and appears here with substantial alterations. Portions of chapter 5 form part of an earlier and much shorter essay published in *Recharting the Thirties*, ed. Patrick M. Quinn (Cranbury, NJ: Associated University Presses, 1995).

Prologue

To say that no sign signifies by itself, that language always refers back to language because at any moment only a few signs are received, is also to say that language is expressive as much through what is *between* the words as through the words themselves, and through what it does not say as much as what it says; just as the painter paints as much by what he traces, by the blanks he leaves, or by the brush marks that he does not make.

Maurice Merleau-Ponty, *The Prose of the World*

If the 1970s retrospectively seem to have set the stage for the victorious emergence of Women's Studies in the Western academy, the 1980s appear to be the decade in which Black, postcolonial and African-American Studies have come into their own as autonomous branches of scholarship, if not integral parts of institutionalized academic thought. A growing diversity of ethnic and multicultural studies have since succeeded in establishing – albeit sometimes precarious – positions in the faculties of arts and social sciences in most contemporary institutions of higher education in both Western Europe and the United States. But while the development of this still expanding and diversifying field continues to provoke debates about its integration into existing curricula, the first half of the 1990s might, at least in some circles, also be recognized as that in which another newcomer made its official début into the world of higher learning. The variegated body of theories and practices making up this newly burgeoning field will, in the context of this book, be provisionally subsumed under the heading of lesbian (and gay) studies, with specific emphasis on the humanities.

The multiplication of Lesbian/Gay and Queer Studies programmes in major US and Western European universities, the birth of Queer Nation (as yet largely contained within the boundaries of English-speaking nations), as well as the remarkable upsurge in media attention for lesbian and gay subjects, may lead future historians to depict the early 1990s as the era in which lesbians and gays were granted permission to step out of their subcultural closets in order to take up their roles on the hitherto pervasively heterosexual stage of mainstream (academic) culture. The extent to which lesbian and gay sexualities have gained public visibility and commercial viability – if not official recognition and respectability in substantial sections of contemporary academia – is perhaps best reflected in the growing numbers of learned books on these formerly sensitive, even forbidden, topics, which since the late 1980s have been rolling off not unprestigious university presses. *Lesbian Configurations* aims to contribute to this still-widening stream.

In its initial conception, I wanted to write a book that would present a more or less comprehensive overview of what has been making its way into the academy (and into increasingly lavishly-produced publishers' catalogues) under various banners: lesbian theory and practice, Lesbian Studies, the New Lesbian Criticism, or the lesbian branches of Queer Theory and what Domna C. Stanton has designated the 'new studies of sexuality'.[1] I optimistically envisaged a volume that would give broad if not exhaustive insight into the critical practices and theoretical models that have been shaping the current project of lesbian studies, with a focus on literature and culture. At the same time, I intended to show that, while partly growing out of mainstream academic feminist criticism, lesbian studies' recent bid for relative autonomy and independence from this affiliated field of cultural analysis, which for many of its practitioners had long provided the most viable intellectual home, on the one hand resulted from certain developments within the critical community at large, and on the other occurred in response to the decidedly heterocentrist bias that, despite an unmistakable growth in multicultural and ethnic awareness, continues to ground the majority of feminist thought.

When I began to stake out the possible contents of a book that could introduce the uninitiated reader to this blossoming new field of critical inquiry, lesbian studies constituted a still fairly negotiable range of writings and readings that seemed relatively easily to fit into the structure of a one-volume study. In the course of the last five or six years, however, lesbian and gay studies have grown into a rapidly expanding, broadly interdisciplinary realm of scholarly investigation; a field, moreover, that has begun to generate some of the most radical and influential ideas about the socio-cultural processes of meaning-production to date. As such, gay/lesbian and queer theories have provided a basis for innovative models of thought relevant not only to the growing ranks of lesbian and gay scholars themselves, but also to cultural critics and analysts whose primary political and intellectual focus lies with other, interrelated axes of differentiation, such as gender, 'race', class, and ethnicity. Hence, even though it had been clear from the start that I would restrict myself to lesbian studies only, I found myself facing an impossible task: the sheer interdisciplinary breadth and theoretical scope of what had, it seemed, almost overnight transformed itself from an extremely marginal field of 'special interest' into a flourishing mode of theory and practice at the cutting edge of socio-political and cultural analysis, rendered the idea of a comprehensive overview as much intellectually unviable as it was physically impossible.

Rather than perversely attempting the impossible, and ending up with a book that would inevitably be too sketchy and overly generalizing to be of any use to even the most maverick students of lesbian criticism and culture, I chose to organize my material somewhat differently than first intended. What follows, then, are a series of chapters that more or less stand by themselves, but that also form constitutive parts in an ongoing investigation of those critical and theoretical issues that lie at the heart of lesbian cultural studies today.

Lesbian Configurations sets out to explore and further develop those enabling ideas coming out of recent lesbian theoretical work that appear most promising for the present and future practice of lesbian scholarship. To realize this overall objective, individual chapters largely retain their basis in the detailed textual analyses in which they find their starting-point. Most centre on specific literary or cinematographic texts, in order to zoom in on certain theoretical questions more directly, or otherwise to engage variously interrelated bodies of thought. Chapters do not all conform to the same format or run to the same length, nor do they approach their subject matter in exactly the same manner. All, however, find common ground in the fact that the book as a whole is centrally concerned with critically investigating the theoretical as well as political potential of a distinctly lesbian mode of cultural analysis and social critique. Furthermore, I have throughout sustained a line of inquiry that forms the second, though not necessarily secondary, preoccupation underlying the project's general scheme: by giving voice to and reflecting on my own, often apprehensive and sometimes downright suspicious reactions to the ways in which popular Western culture has recently been tapping in on the 'voguing' of queerness. In other words, as well as showing the potential of lesbian theory in practice, and probing its liberatory force within the larger project of radical socio-cultural critique, I hope to shed some light on what seems a less fortunate aspect of the coming-out of queerness in the academy, that is, the striking side-show of popular 'lesbian' figures and images that has gradually been emerging along with the waxing stream of critical discourse on the subject of lesbianism – a subject, one might almost forget, that only a few years ago was as invisible as it has traditionally been unspeakable.

In her aptly entitled book, *The Apparitional Lesbian*, Terry Castle argues that the 'literary history of lesbianism . . . is first of all a history of derealization.' Tracing its inscription in Western art and literature through the eighteenth and nineteenth centuries, she remarks that lesbianism, or even its possibility, 'can only be represented to the degree that it is simultaneously "derealized" ', made to disappear from view through the 'infusion of spectral metaphors':

> One woman or the other must be a ghost, or on the way to becoming one. Passion is excited, only to be obscured, disembodied, decarnalized. The vision is inevitably waved off. Panic seems to underwrite these obsessional spectralizing gestures: a panic over love, female pleasure, and the possibility of women breaking free – together – from their male overseers. Homophobia is the order of the day, entertains itself (wryly or gothically) with phantoms, then exorcizes them.[2]

If such a description of the lesbian's ephemeral existence, its characterization in terms of 'ghosting', seems pertinent to Western art and literature of earlier centuries, it has by no means lost its significance in the present day. Castle's focus is, in this instance, on French male-authored texts originating in the eighteenth century. In this book, in contrast, I will concentrate on twentieth-century reincarnations of this 'spectral lesbian', and on the continuous re-inscription of lesbian sexuality and desire as a 'phantasmatic enterprise'.[3] To demonstrate that the recreation of such 'ghostly' incarnations is neither the prerogative of the male imagination, nor restricted to either the popular or the more traditionally literary domain, the specific appearance of the elusive lesbian figure is interrogated in both male- and female-authored texts. While some of these texts have become part of the established canon, though largely on different grounds, others, far from being recognized as in some way or other classifiable as 'lesbian' will be less familiar, or perhaps completely unknown to most readers.

Chapter 1 stakes out some of the aims and the specific potential of lesbian cultural criticism. Using the contested status of Alice Walker's best-selling novel *The Color Purple* (1982) as a starting-point, the chapter begins by raising the question of definition. What makes a text into a lesbian one? Must the author be a lesbian to make it so? And what if she is 'known' to be a lesbian, but does not explicitly deal with the subject in her work? Does that still qualify as 'lesbian'? And what about language? Does sexuality enter into the ways we speak and write? Is there such a thing as lesbian writing, even a lesbian aesthetic, as distinct from a gay male, a female or feminist one? And finally, how are we to approach the role of the reader/critic? To what extent do critics determine what counts as lesbian and what not? And if they do, does this mean that any text may be read from a lesbian perspective?[4] A brief analysis of the ambivalent procedures by which lesbian desire is narrativized in Walker's novel aims to illustrate what such a perspective may entail, revealing that the mere presence of lesbian characters, or a thematic focus on lesbian desire, does not necessarily prevent a text from effecting precisely the kind of 'exorcizing' process by which the lesbian figure ultimately evaporates. Or, in Castle's terms, by which lesbian love, sexuality and desire are at once 'disembodied' and 'decarnalized'.

Appearances to the contrary notwithstanding, that the process of 'ghosting' to which the lesbian has historically been subjected has hardly subsided today will become even clearer in chapters 2 and 3. These chapters critically engage with recent (male-directed) films in which female same-sex desire is centrally invoked only to be obscured and, eventually, violently eradicated. Starting with a theoretical discussion of the lesbian's in/visibility in Western culture at large, chapter 2 concentrates on the material inscription of such in/visibility in a representative example of 'lesbian' imagery in contemporary Hollywood cinema, the controversial sexual thriller *Basic Instinct* (1992), directed by the Dutch filmmaker Paul Verhoeven. At the time of its release Verhoeven's first international success provoked a great deal of debate, both in the mainstream media and in various segments of the gay community. The main focus of debate was the extremely hostile way in which the film represents its (extraordinarily large) cast of lesbian characters. Rather than reiterating such critiques – which, in fact, would amount to no more than stating the obvious – my discussion serves to bring to light the less obvious ways in which *Basic Instinct* succeeds in reinscribing earlier 'spectralizing gestures' with regard to the lesbian, and thus, despite its postmodern gloss, continues a tradition of 'ghosting' that goes back at least as far as the seventeenth century.

Revealing the pervasiveness of this mainstream cultural tradition, and showing that homo-, or rather, lesbophobia is still the order of the day, not just within the notoriously phobic and panic-driven realm of the Hollywood Dream Machine, chapter 3 presents a critical analysis of a less well-known European film, *Bitter Moon* (1992), directed by Roman Polanski. Expanding on a line of argument developed in the preceding chapter, the discussion of this deceptively self-reflexive narrative of anxious masculinity, rather than focusing on the fearful fascination of the cultural 'malestream' with female same-sex desire *per se*, concentrates more particularly on the significance of the lesbian as a figure of Otherness in a hegemonic (straight white male) cultural imaginary that finds itself increasingly under threat in our postmodern, multicultural times.

Dominant and non-dominant forms of cultural production may be differently situated in the larger socio-symbolic realm; both are inevitably bound to the restrictive as well as the enabling operations of prevailing signifying processes. It is not surprising therefore to find that female authors, past and present, have used strategies of revelation and concealment not dissimilar to those employed by their male counterparts in articulating lesbian desire or presenting lesbian characters in their work. This is not to say that the strategies of 'derealization' that serve to obliterate the threat of female same-sex desire in most male-authored texts are merely copied or employed in exactly the same way or, by extension, to the same effect in cultural production bearing a woman's signature. Censorship laws and fear of social disapprobation have forced many lesbian writers in the past to deal with their scandalous subject in masked or coded terms. Some of these texts manifest an internalized lesbophobia that underlines the overwhelming impact of dominant ideologies of sex and sexuality on even the most intellectually acute and otherwise self-aware of twentieth-century women writers and artists. Others, in contrast, display a striking ingenuity in sidestepping the rules of silence and invisibility that have traditionally determined the lesbian's cultural role. Working around the edges of language, they have succeeded in creating a variety of symbolic markers – sustained patterns of imagery, metaphors, personal names, and other tropes – that are at once recognizable as expressions of the 'love that dare not speak its name' to those who know how to read them, but that look innocent enough to pass the attention of censors and other, less knowledgeable readers.

The extent to which female authors are capable of *self-consciously* employing such strategies of disclosure and concealment, in order to articulate some form of lesbian desire, varies considerably, being largely dependent on the socio-historical context in which they are situated and within which they write. Chapters 4 and 5 demonstrate such differences. Moving away from both the contemporary scene and the motion picture, each chapter explores configurations of lesbian sexuality in literary texts written by women, originating in highly distinct socio-cultural moments in twentieth-century Western history. Close textual analyses make it clear that attitudes towards sex and sexuality generally, and towards lesbian sexuality in particular, have not, in the course of the century that is now drawing to its close, developed in a progressive line of increasing liberation.[5] While a general loosening up of traditional sexual taboos is unmistakably part of larger socio-historical developments in modern Western societies, lesbianism, it appears, has not equally enjoyed growing visibility and social acceptability. Indeed, by reversing the chronological order in which they originally appeared in discussing these texts, I seek to underscore such discontinuity. But apart from showing the discontinuities in the history of lesbian representation that have occurred since the sexualization of the socio-cultural domain at the turn of the century up until the emergence of the women's liberation and gay and lesbian movements in the late 1960s, my purpose in this section is to illustrate how deconstructive theoretical tools may be constructively deployed and utilized in a practice of 'symptomatic' lesbian reading. In other words, to show how recently developed critical tools may be employed 'anachronistically' in order to wrest unsaid – or indeed unsayable – sexual meanings from seemingly straightforward, pre-liberation texts.

Chapter 4 offers such a 'perverse' reading of Sylvia Plath's *The Bell Jar* (1963), a novel whose legendary status largely derives from what has usually been read as a horrifying, and implicitly heterosexual, inscription of 'beset womanhood' in McCarthy's America. Jumping across the Atlantic Ocean and thirty years back in time, chapter 5, in contrast, centres on a short novel written in England in the first half of this century, *Friends and Relations* (1931) by the Anglo-Irish writer Elizabeth Bowen. Apart from highlighting the historically determined differences in the ways in which women writers have attempted simultaneously to express and to conceal female same-sex desire in eras preceding 'second wave' feminism and gay liberation, the chapter interrogates the long-standing association of lesbianism with textual figurations of female adolescence.

Veering away from the 'literary' and interpretive mode of the foregoing inquiries, chapter 6 resumes and continues various theoretical conversations initiated in earlier sections. Picking up on an issue briefly commented upon in chapter 1, and thus bringing the line of this book's narrative quest full circle, my main concern

in this chapter is the difficult relationship between feminist critical discourse and lesbian cultural studies. First, the complexities
and barely disguised tensions that have characterized the relations between lesbianism and feminism from the early 1970s
onwards are subjected to critical scrutiny. Drawing on a selection
of both feminist and lesbian writings, the complex causes underlying the strained relations between these affiliated fields of study
are further explored from the perspective of (neo)-Freudian and
(neo)-Lacanian psychoanalytic theory, in order to shed some light
on the underlying grounds of such complexities. Following closely
upon the line of argument set out here, the epilogue briefly out-
lines a notion of lesbian scholarship as a mode of 'participative
thinking,' as a practice of thought and of everyday life, which, in
interrelation with other politically informed modes of cultural
analysis, may help us better to perceive some of the significant
blanks lining the Western collective imagination. As a specific
form of participative thinking, lesbian cultural criticism, I ultimately argue, enables us more fully to read those cultural expressions of sexuality that speak, to recall Merleau-Ponty's words, 'as
much through what is *between* the words as through the words
themselves'. By allowing us to understand, at least to some
extent, what those 'ghostly' yet significant spaces in between the
terms of gendered heterosexuality may mean, the radical potential of lesbian critical theory and practice may – as I hope this
book will succeed in conveying – yet turn out to be indispensable,
not only to lesbian critics and theorists, but also to practitioners
of cultural analysis in general.

1 Defining Differences: The Lavender Menace and *The Color Purple*

It would be incorrect to say that lesbians associate, make love, live with other women, for 'woman' has meaning only in heterosexual systems of thought and heterosexual economic systems. Lesbians are not women.

Monique Wittig, 'The Straight Mind'

Monique Wittig's controversial proclamations concerning the lesbian's essential difference from other female subjects continue to provoke ardent debate. The apparently counter-intuitive sway of the phrase 'Lesbians are not women', nonetheless lands us squarely with the – as far as lesbian sexuality is concerned – inevitable problematics of definition and demarcation. If lesbians are not women, what are they? Indeed, to shift our focus to the realm of culture, what could qualify as lesbian cultural production, whether it be literature, music, painting, and cinema, or some other, less officially acknowledged form, such as privately produced videos, comic books, parlour plays, charades, and performance art? Or to narrow down the question even further: how to define the lesbian quality of a single cultural text, especially when such a text emphatically engages more than the subject of lesbian sexuality only? Alice Walker's *The Color Purple* (1982) would appear to present a sufficiently challenging case to trace the implications of these interrelated questions.

Is *The Color Purple* a black novel, a feminist novel, or a lesbian one? Does its publication to wide critical acclaim and subsequent commercial success represent a landmark in the respective traditions of feminist, African-American or lesbian fiction? To frame the problem somewhat differently: can Walker's prize-winning novel be justifiably 'claimed' by feminist, black or lesbian critics? That it would be impossible to answer any of these questions once and for all does not mean that they are merely silly, even irrelevant ones. For what they point up is that questions of meaning are never simple, and that different readers bring different histories and experiences to texts, which in turn will give rise to different answers. But as questions of definition, they also alert us to a problem that directly affects the subject of this book, lesbian sexuality in the field of culture – or, conversely, the study of culture from what I will, provisionally, call a lesbian perspective. To illustrate what such a perspective may entail, my purpose in this chapter is to offer a lesbian reading of *The Color Purple*, setting off my remarks against those of several of Walker's earlier critics, and thus begin to unravel the questions of definition outlined above. In order to do so, I must first make a brief excursion into history.

In the late 1960s, with the rise of various new social movements, among which black, women's and gay liberation groups figure most prominently, the word lesbian began to acquire newly political significance. From a merely stigmatizing label, 'lesbian' became a positive term of self-identification as well as a banner for social organization and radical political action. From the start, lesbianism was closely associated with feminism, if only because the sheer existence of lesbians proved that Women's Liberation was not just a utopian fantasy. As sexual 'deviants', lesbians had, after all, long been living their lives in a way that became central to the early feminist dream, that is to say, in financial, emotional, and sexual independence from men. That the responsibilities such independence entailed were largely on a par with those of the upholders of patriarchal society did not mean that lesbians shared the same privileges as men. Lesbians and feminists initially found a common cause in the struggle for the equal civil rights that, due to their gender, were denied to both.

The threat of lesbianism, consisting in precisely this sexual and social autonomy, was rapidly seized upon and used by anti-feminist forces which saw their former privileges challenged by the unfeminine ideas and disruptive politics of the Women's Liberation Movement. The dominant media generally depicted feminists as a bunch of man-hating, bra-burning lesbians, too ugly and frustrated to gain – or indeed, deserve – (the love of) men.[1] Many heterosexual feminists feared that the association would prove counter-productive to their fight for social reform, and insisted that the lesbian input of the movement was both publicly and privately played down. Such internalized homo- or, more correctly, lesbophobia, caused Betty Friedan, founder of the National Organization of Women (NOW) in the US, to reject the 'insult' of lesbianism on national television. Denounced as the 'lavender menace' that would harm the overall feminist cause, NOW's lesbian members were subsequently systematically expelled.[2] It would take two years of bitter feud for NOW to change its policy, and to incorporate lesbian rights into its legislative agenda. While strictly speaking an American affair, the NOW/Lavender Menace controversy was representative of attitudes towards lesbianism prevailing within many branches of the women's movement, also outside the US.[3]

It was no accident that Betty Friedan referred to the lesbian membership she feared would 'discredit' the National Organisation of Women as the 'lavender menace'. The colours violet and lavender have a history of association with lesbianism that goes as far back as 600 BC, to the poet Sappho and her female lovers who reputedly wore violet tiaras in their hair. By choosing *The Color Purple* as a title for her novel, Alice Walker, without actually having to utter the 'forbidden' word, implicitly – yet unmistakably – places the issue of lesbian sexuality at the focus of her narrative, as well as at the centre of Celie's epistolary coming-into-being. Such centrality has, however, not been generally acknowledged in the novel's popular reception. Indeed, one may well ask if *The Color Purple* would have gained its immediate and widespread public acceptance – winning both the Pulitzer Prize in 1983 and the American Book Award for 1982–3 – had Walker been more unequivocal in rendering the protagonist's perverse desires the heart and core of her success story.

As it is, Walker's text proved sufficiently ambivalent to accommodate Steven Spielberg's highly sanitized film adaptation, the Hollywood blockbuster of the same title, in which the aspect of lesbian sexuality is both displaced from the centre of narrative events and virtually rendered invisible so as not to risk offending its targeted mass audience.[4] But whereas the film has been criticized for its romanticization of a harrowing story of sexual violence, female oppression and father/daughter incest, in addition to being attacked for practically erasing the issue of lesbian desire, Walker's novel has primarily been taken to task, not exclusively but particularly by feminist critics, on different grounds.

Perhaps the most frequently criticized aspect of *The Color Purple* is its pastoral quality, its presentation of a romanticized rural community in an imaginary South inhabited by a cast of stock characters who, in the end, miraculously blend together in a utopian vision of metaphysical unity. Dismissed as an altogether 'unrealistic' representation of post-Civil War life as it was lived by the majority of black people, and especially black women, in the former slave states of the USA, Walker's evocation of the South as a pastoral realm in which (victimized) female characters ultimately attain both social and sexual self-fulfilment, while (abusive) male characters undergo moral and spiritual conversion, has been castigated for downplaying the harsh realities of African-American lives under the equal sway of racist and sexist oppression. In an early essay, Cora Kaplan, situating herself as an 'American expatriate who has taught literature and history in a British university for fifteen ... years of voluntary exile', persuasively argues against such reductionist readings of the novel.[5] Knowing from classroom experience that it is particularly difficult to 'get across' to white European readers both the structural role of racism in contemporary US society and an understanding of the specificities of the internal feuds and conflicts that have continued to divide Black social and political movements since the 1950s and 1960s, she insists on the critical and political need to place *The Color Purple* in its proper context.

The particularities of Walker's text, especially its presumed failure to meet the standards of classical realist fiction – still generally upheld as the unquestioned hallmark of Great Literature in the Western Academy – should, Kaplan suggests, instead of being dismissed as stylistic flaws, be regarded as a conscious inscription in a tradition of Black female writing stretching back to the nineteenth century. From the boost in Black writing during the 1920s and 1930s known as the 'Harlem Renaissance', to the polemic of Black men writing in the 1950s and 1960s, female Black writers have, she maintains, been engaged in 'fierce intimate dialogue with that writing and its androcentric politics'.[6] Moreover, Black women writers coming into prominence in the 1970s and 1980s, among them Toni Morrison, Toni Cade Bambara, Audre Lorde, Paule Marshall, and Walker herself, not only affirmed the powerful influence of older Black female authors such as Zora Neale Hurston and Gwendolyn Brooks, but also insisted on actively carrying on debates with white feminists about the 'ways in which American feminism, past and present, has been deeply complicit with racism'. These contradictory and conflictual histories are necessarily reflected in a style of writing that, Kaplan proposes, not so much fails to comply with literary convention but consciously refuses to use 'updated versions of classical realist forms'.[7]

One set of texts that serves as such a 'dialogizing background' to *The Color Purple* are the Southern writings of celebrated Black male novelists such as Richard Wright and Ralph Ellison (James Baldwin being somewhat of an exception). Both Wright's *Black Boy* (1945) and Ellison's *Invisible Man* (1952), Kaplan maintains, focus 'on the imperilled masculinity of Black men', reconstructing an imaginary Southern rural community in which women are presented as 'either powerless or repressive'. By setting up a reconstructed family structure, in which women are neither powerless nor reduced to mere objects of (male) abuse but are, instead, presented as active agents in the network of social relations underpinning an – equally imaginary – Southern rural community, *The Color Purple*, Kaplan argues, should be seen as a 'more optimistic "sequel" ' to its male pre-texts, offering a 'paradigm of change through the agency of Black women'. Its 'utopianism' is thus rather less simple than an insufficiently contextualized reading may suggest. Seen as a 'polemic against the deeply negative imaginative interpretations of southern Black life in much male black fiction and autobiography', Walker's controversial text, Kaplan therefore concludes, projects a 'dynamic version of Black female subjectivity that, in effect, rewrites its representations as they appear in both white and Black, male and female southern fictions.'[8]

British critic Alison Light also remarks upon the difficulties *The Color Purple* poses to white (feminist) readers, especially to those readers who position themselves on the left of the political spectrum, with its longstanding tradition of 'countercriticism', and a concurrent, almost exclusive emphasis on 'struggle, strife, and conflict'. How, Light pointedly asks, is a white feminist critic to reconcile Walker's (and her heroine's) success story and its achievement of happiness, harmony, and self-affirmation, with her own self-appointed task of reading texts against the grain? How is she to negotiate between Walker's utopian visions and her own need to expose popular culture's 'complicity with dominant ideas and values', the oppressive structures of meaning that such a critic perceives as harmful to women, blacks, and other minority groups alike? While arguing that it is precisely the novel's jubilantly harmonious, happy ending that accounts for its almost universal appeal, its best-selling success, Light warns against reading such appeal in universalistic, non-differentiated ways. Celie's story, she suggests, does not mean the same thing to all audiences. In fact, where the rules of left-wing 'political correctness' may lead white feminist readers to reject the novel's successful resolution as an uncritical, apolitical reinforcement of the liberal humanist values that sustain an oppressive dominant culture, such an appropriation of possibilities for (self) fulfilment in a modern-day 'slave narrative' might well signify a radical, indeed, subversive gesture to members of non-white, non-middle-class, and otherwise disenfranchized reading audiences.

There is, however, another level on which Light considers dismissing Walker's unifying vision as overly optimistic or naïve critically unwarranted. Even if the 'dream of full achievement' as materialized in the novel may have different meanings for different groups of readers, there is, or so she maintains, a 'bottom level at which *The Color Purple* keys into a far more diffuse desire for personal and social changes . . . . an appeal to the possibility of amelioration, of "progress", which is no less potent or mobilizing for being an imaginary vision, a happy ending still to come.'[9] In this sense, and here Light underscores Kaplan's earlier suggestions, the novel's 'utopianism' can only be considered problematic if it is read from a social realist perspective – a perspective that not only fails to do justice to this particular novel, but which is, in the final instance, a reductive, even inappropriate approach to fiction in general. For as Light quite rightly points out, to the extent that fiction does not coincide with 'real life', it is not only ineluctably imaginary, but, in effect, *by definition* in excess of life as it is lived in daily reality. All fiction, then, could be said to be 'utopian – though some more than others'. Rather than a sentimental, and thus not sufficiently politically informed, popular novel, Light suggests that we view Celie's story as an 'enabling dream', a fantasy in which the tensions between (under-privileged) readers' struggles for self-fulfilment in their real lives and the 'happy ending still to come' are productively exploited to present the possibility of individual, and especially (black) female, agency. It is only by choosing to tell her story in the form of a romantic fairy tale that Walker is able to present a 'dream of full achievement, of a world in which all conflicts and contradictions are resolved'.[10]

In their respective investigations of the underlying assumptions of white (feminist) critiques of *The Color Purple*, both Kaplan and Light raise important points about the critical reception of Black texts by white audiences generally, and about the overall 'colour-blindness' of established practices of academic criticism in particular. While correctly taking white readers to task for failing to take fully into account how ethnic and racial differentiation 'colours' our views and hence our critical and theoretical practices, these same critics, however, show very little awareness of the ways in which differences in sexuality equally structure the perspectives from which both black and white readers approach literary texts. Both duly mention, though rather fleetingly and almost in passing, that Celie's sexual awakening does not follow the 'normal', heterosexual path inscribed in a tradition of female novels of development, starting with Kate Chopin's classic female *Bildungsroman, The Awakening* (1899). Both equally fail, however, to address the specificity of the protagonist's 'abnormal', lesbian desires. For what, in effect, is a lesbian reader to make of Light's observation that 'Celie gets it all in the end of the story'? Is Celie's epistolary coming-into-being indeed a romantic fairy tale of utopian dimensions, an 'enabling dream', when seen from a lesbian point of view? Or, to come back to the questions I began with, is *The Color Purple* a lesbian novel? Does it belong to a lesbian cultural tradition? And how would a contemporary lesbian critic go about answering such questions? Different theoretical moments would no doubt generate different answers, depending on the critical aims and terminological tools used by individual readers/critics. My ambivalence about calling *The Color Purple* a lesbian novel does not, however, merely reflect the inevitable partiality of any critical approach or theoretical perspective. Such equivocations as I have primarily issue from an unequivocal sense of ambivalence both produced by and inscribed in the text itself.

Thematically, in terms of characterization and as far as narrative development is concerned, I would say, yes, *The Color Purple* is definitely a lesbian novel. Celie's struggle against patriarchal power, her gradual acquisition of a position of sexual autonomy, and her eventual socio-economic independence, all form clearly recognizable aspects, or stages, in an established tradition of lesbian stories of development or *Bildungsromane*.[11] That Celie's story is outspokenly lesbian, and not just any woman's coming-to-consciousness, is underlined by the precise nature of the dynamic force that causes its (and her) development. This is not to deny that the novel shares many characteristics with other narratives of female empowerment: in addition to the overall story-line, we might point to the fact that the central characters are all female, that the protagonist's only 'nurturing' or, better, non-destructive relationships are with other women, and remark its triumphantly 'liberatory' conclusion. These features, however, do nothing to diminish the pivotal significance of what lies at the novel's narrative core: the heroine's discovery of her *lesbian* sexuality.

The Color Purple's plot is not triggered off by the protagonist's discovery of her sexuality regardless of its orientation, as many feminists have argued. The moment of narrative combustion, Celie's moment of 'awakening' is emphatically rendered as a non-normatively 'female', that is, a *lesbian* moment of self-discovery. In the letters that make up the first half of the text, the force of her same-sex desire for Shug is thematically underscored by being frequently, explicitly remarked upon. Foregrounding the overtly physical nature of their relationship, the text throughout highlights the experience of lesbian sex in furthering and sustaining the process of the heroine's burgeoning subjectivity. Such central-ity is underlined by the interconnected meanings of the novel's title. The colour purple literally refers to a field of flowers that comes to symbolize the protagonist's rejection of God as a white male authority and his transformation into a non-Christian, de-personalised spiritual force. On a metaphorical level, however, the colour purple, with its longstanding tradition of associations, signifies sex between Celie and Shug, and lesbianism generally. This suggests that it is only as a lesbian, that is to say, in her emotional, intellectual *and* sexual independence from men, that Celie can become an autonomous subject, the author of her own perceptions, and ultimately, of her own discourse.

Lesbian desire in *The Color Purple* is thus not accidental to the overarching plot of female development, or a somewhat peculiar private preference on the part of the protagonist. Since nothing in novels – unlike real life – is either incidental or unpremeditated, Celie does not simply 'happen to fall in love' with a woman. Her sexual orientation, her passionate investment in a female Other from whom she gradually begins to derive her sense of Self, struc-turally informs the story of her subjectivity, her empowerment as a subject of speech and writing, and eventually also as a social agent. Explicit recognition of the narrative focus on Celie's 'deviant' sexuality may, at least partly, solve one of the problems critics of the novel have been struggling with, i.e., the relative absence of the question of 'race' as an area of problematization. In other words, the fact that all the 'bad guys' are black men, whose significance, just as that of their female counterparts, is confined to the black community, and not taken out into the wider context provided by the racist society of the American South.[12] Seen from a lesbian perspective, this is not necessarily a political or critical flaw, but rather an indication of the fact that 'race' does not stand, at least not exclusively, at the novel's narrative and thematic centre.

A lesbian approach also helps to explain a further, otherwise unresolvable, problem posed by the text, one with which feminist critics in particular have continued to struggle: Celie's 'inexpli-cable' mildness, even benevolence towards Mr.- at the end of the story. Only if we acknowledge the structural importance of the fact that it is Shug, another woman, who constitutes the object of

Celie's desires, and who, in the course of time, acquires the function of 'significant Other' to the heroine's Self, are we able to see that the latter's relations with Mr.-, and men generally, are of a nature best described in terms of complete *in*difference. Celie's subjectivity does not depend on her interrelations with men or, more generally, on assuming her place in male-defined institutions. On the contrary, her budding sense of identity and emergence as a subjective agent are precisely enabled by her rejection of the role prescribed to her in the patriarchal script of gendered heterosexuality. Since she does not rely on a male Other to differentiate her Self, the protagonist has, in the end, nothing to lose or to gain from being 'nice' to Mr.-. Positioned outside the socio-symbolic ring in which the battle between the sexes is traditionally most savagely fought out, that is, the domain of (hetero)sexuality, Celie occupies an ex-centric position in the sex-gender system, from which she can afford to be generously indifferent to members of the opposite sex.

With such evidence to the contrary, why do I still hesitate to call *The Color Purple* a lesbian text? Why not embrace Walker's novel as a welcome addition to a still largely white lesbian canon? My reluctance to do so does not, it will be clear, revolve around the question of whether or not lesbian sexuality figures (sufficiently) prominently in the text. Rather, such reservations pertain to the manner in which the lesbian subject is dealt with, especially in the latter half of the novel. In one of the (to my knowledge) few critical essays that does explicitly address the question of sexuality, bell hooks rightly contends that one of the problematic aspects of *The Color Purple* resides in the fundamental de-politicization of lesbianism it insists on establishing.[13] Gainsaying the proverbial, yet palpably real homophobia pervasively reigning within Western social reality, perhaps even more so in the black community, Celie and Shug can apparently openly carry on having a sexual relationship, without causing so much as a ripple within the heterosexual order. As hooks correctly points out: 'Homophobia does not exist in the novel.'[14] This is not only quite odd in a narrative that, despite its overall surreal atmosphere, emphatically inscribes itself in the tradition of social realism. It also entails that Celie's perverse desires – by which the process of her subjectivity itself is set in motion – remain an ultimately private affair. Unlike her entrepreneurial activities, and her eventual role as a house- and landowner, the heroine's sexuality does not obtain in any social or even collective context. Since there is no social reality in which she can express her desires, Celie's choice of a female love object carries no meaning outside her relationship with Shug.

Its reduction to a matter of private preference represents not only a de-politicization of lesbian sexuality *per se*, it also implies that Celie's sexuality has no significance outside the privacy of the bedroom in which she and Shug perform their perverse practices. Hence, once Shug betrays her to return to the normal order of (unhappy) heterosexuality, Celie does not merely stop having sex, she stops being a sexual subject altogether. Lacking any collective sense of lesbian identity, Shug's leaving her means the end of the perverse performance of her subjectivity as a whole. The residues of the heroine's de-sexualized self become subsequently inscribed in the 'masculine' accoutrements belonging to the stereotypical 'mythic mannish lesbian'.[15] Celie may in the end be wearing the pants around the house, but that is indeed the only remaining marker of her subversive sexuality. Collapsing the threadbare image of the 'mannish lesbian' with the equally stereotypical view of lesbianism as a harmless, or sexually-innocent, form of sororal affection, the text eventually succeeds in conclusively neutralizing Celie's 'abnormal' desire by implying its integration into love of kin, in particular for her sister Nettie. The potentially subversive force of the heroine's newly acquired sense of self is thus contained within the traditional family structure – however strangely assorted a group Celie's 'family' members in the novel's closing section may seem to make up.

Celie's is not, however, the only character to be effectively robbed of its radical edge. Shug, too, is unmistakably stripped of the autonomous sexual power that has constituted her character's defining feature from the start. When she leaves Celie for a man half her age, it is not because she is lusting after a new sexual adventure. On the contrary, prior to this final venture into the heterosexual market, the formerly so glamorous, autonomous female is recurrently portrayed as a fat, aging woman, fearful of losing her looks, and therewith the only means she has to wield power (over men). Given the matter-of-fact, even dispassionate tone of voice in which Shug's erotic disempowerment is depicted, it comes as no surprise that, after a brief fling with the adorable young musician of her desperate choice, she fails to hold his erotic attention, and instead of playing his lover, ends up performing a more 'appropriate' role as his substitute mother.

Shug's degrading heterosexualization strikes me as an altogether uncalled-for turn of events within the narrative context of *The Color Purple* as a whole. What I find most disturbing about the character's demeaning restoration to the heterosexual order, however, is the fact that it is presented, without a trace of narrative critique, as the inevitable conclusion to a – perhaps unusually active – career of (hetero)sexual womanhood. In other words, what is essentially a thorough devaluation of her character, indeed, the end of Shug as an autonomously operating socio-sexual agent, is uncritically held up as the female subject's ineluctable fate in the 'natural' order of things; an oppressive socio-symbolic order the novel itself in the end takes great pains to restore.

Celie's de-sexualization and Shug's socio-sexual disempowerment jointly constitute a narrative divestiture of female agency which coincides with, if it has not actually been brought about by, the breaking-off of their sexual relations. Taken together, the respective situations in which we leave the two central characters, plus the fact that the novel nonetheless ends on a happy note of harmony, of restoration, substantially undermine *The Color Purple*'s subversive potential as a feminist, an African-American, but also as a lesbian text.

As we have seen, some critics have rejected Walker's celebrated bestseller for its lack of realism, its enforced and unconvincing happy ending, in short, for being more of a romantic fairy tale than a critical piece of realist fiction. To counter such dismissive gestures, Alison Light, in the essay referred to above, aptly comments upon the racial and ethnic indifference that characterizes white academic practices. She hence correctly (self-consciously) observes that is 'often the case that only those who take privileges and comfort for granted' are 'unable to learn that different lives produce their own equally important forms of knowledge and community – knowledge, from which they are by definition excluded'.[16] Seen in the light of my (lesbian) reading of the text, it seems to me that it is precisely such exclusion from a different sexual – as distinct from a racial or ethnic – community, that allows Light and other non-lesbian critics, feminist and otherwise, to hail Walker's text as the fulfilment of an altogether 'enabling dream'. As a lesbian reader, I perhaps primarily find fault with the novel for its failure to be precisely that: a romantic fairy tale. Fairy tales, as Light quite rightly emphasizes, have of old offered both readers and writers opportunities to freely range the never-never land of their wildest fantasies. As my foregoing comments seek to convey, to me, as a lesbian reader, *The Color Purple* precludes such possibilities. In my imaginary, ideal lesbian fairy tale, the fantastic, alluring and unregenerately lesbian lovers would not be stripped of their life-giving force so as to be brought back into a very real, heterosexual order: they would, quite extraordinarily, end up living happily ever after. But the widespread public acceptance of such a story was, in 1982, perhaps too much of a 'happy ending still to come'. In the next chapter we shall see if this still holds true exactly a decade later.

2 Basic Instinct: The Lesbian Spectre as Castrating Agent

> The lesbian vampire is the most powerful representation of lesbianism to be found on the commercial movie screen, and rather than abandon her for what she signifies, it may be possible to extricate her from her original function, and reappropriate her power.
>
> Andrea Weiss, *Vampires and Violets*

The lesbian made her formal début in Anglo-Saxon culture by appearing in the *Shorter Oxford English Dictionary* (*SOED*) in 1908. The brief entry on this newcomer on the stage of Western sexuality, as it still reads in the 1986 edition of this venerable volume, gives us the following two definitions: 1. Of or pertaining to the island of Lesbos; 2. *Lesbian vice*, Sapphism. These somewhat elusive descriptions are supplemented with an even more obscure reference to something called a 'lesbian rule', which is stated to denote a 'mason's rule made of lead', and, in its figurative sense, 'a pliant principle of judgement'. While the latter in particular offers itself up to 'perverse' reappropriation, the seemingly auspicious entry of the 'lesbian' into the official language set the terms for a history of linguistic circumvention that continues to this very day. Rather than giving lesbianism its place on the discursive map in the sense in which most current speakers of English would understand the term, the *SOED* created a space for female same-sex desire not so much as a visible and recognizable cultural presence, but rather as a discursive absence, as a cognitive gap within the conceptual scheme underpinning the power structures of social reality, not just in Anglo-America, but in the Western world at large.

Subsumed under the category of the 'Third Sex' within the early sexological discourses emerging in the second half of the nineteenth century,[1] the curious figure of the 'female homosexual' pursued her career as a negative semantic space in heteropatriarchal culture in what was, in the course of the twentieth century, to become the leading theory of sexuality, Freudian psychoanalysis. While radically innovative in many other respects, Freud betrays his nineteenth-century roots in similarly hiding female same-sex desire behind the screen of the (sexological) notion of gender-inversion.[2] Even within the space carved out more recently by feminist discourses on 'sexual difference', in the sense of woman's difference from man, the lesbian merely haunts the edges of the field of vision. Feminist models of thought remain within the confines of the phallocentric Law insofar as the presence/absence of the phallus continues to constitute the primary organizing principle of their theories of gender. Such critiques hence effectively reinscribe dominant cultural scenarios in which the female subject can function only as Other to the male/Same. To the extent, then, that the majority of both dominant and reverse-discourses, such as feminism, take the notion of a binary, oppositional sexual difference as their starting-point, lesbian invisibility is inscribed in the very coordinates of the phallocentric conceptual realm equally underlying them. In the final analysis, 'sexual difference' is, as Teresa de Lauretis has pointed out, essentially the term of a 'sexual indifference', a model of gendered desire in which 'female desire for the self-same, another female self, cannot be recognized.'[3]

An excluded Other in the dominant cultural tradition, the lesbian subject is, or so maintained feminist philosopher Sara Hoagland almost twenty years ago, placed 'in the interesting and peculiar position of being something that doesn't exist'. Whilst such exclusion from the general scheme of things has, as we have already seen, led to a problem of definition which continues to preoccupy lesbian theorists, this same conceptual impossibility, Hoagland suggests, provides the lesbian subject with a 'singular vantage point with respect to the reality which does not include her'. Enjoying a 'certain freedom from constraints of the conceptual system', the elusive subject is argued to have 'access to knowledge which is inaccessible to those whose existence *is* countenanced by the system'. The lesbian theorist would therefore be able to 'undertake kinds of criticism and description, and intellectual invention, hitherto unimagined'.[4]

In the light of these rather unusual claims with regard to a historically largely invisible minority group, the intriguing reference in the *SOED* to a 'lesbian rule' as a 'pliant principle of judgement' would appear to take on unexpected epistemological significance. But whatever the implications of the subversive intellectual powers this storehouse of official knowledge may thus, from the outset, have unwittingly attributed to the practitioners of the mysterious lesbian 'vice', it seems clear that the lesbian's position within the conceptual frame of heteropatriarchy is a profoundly paradoxical one. Not being countenanced by the general scheme of things or, in more theoretical terms, excluded from the socio-symbolic order, the 'female invert' is a figure of cultural invisibility. At the same time, however, she is claimed to be endowed with privileged powers of vision with regard to the culture that refuses to recognize her. These paradoxical attributes, the ostensibly incompatible aspects qualifying the nebulous presence of the lesbian figure on the Western social scene are, it seems to me, not so much mutually exclusive or merely unfortunate effects of historical circumstance. Rather, by viewing the 'impossible' figure's conflicting attributes as interdependent and constitutive parts of an irreducible contradiction – called lesbian sexuality – I wish to approach the paradox of female same-sex desire as a destabilizing knot in the discursive web making up dominant social reality, a moment in the conceptual universe in which questions of knowledge and meaning converge with visions of sexuality and being in a complex, yet potentially revealing, if not subversive manner.

The thoroughness with which lesbianism has been suppressed within thousands of years of Western history, and the persistence with which lesbian experience is denied recognition and visibility in even present-day mainstream cultural practice, cannot be considered accidental. Indeed, as Marilyn Frye has contended, the 'metaphysical overkill' with which the figure of the lesbian is erased from the phallocentric realm of thought indisputably signals a 'manipulation, a scurrying to erase, to divert the eye, the attention, the mind'. And since the 'overdetermination' with which the figure of the lesbian is subjected to processes of cultural concealment and collective disavowal cannot be disassociated from the larger socio-historical context in which these occur, the lesbian's mandatory spectral existence, Frye suggests, 'has to do . . . with the maintenance of phallocratic reality as a whole'.[5]

By invoking the lesbian's cultural invisibility as a potential site of epistemic privilege, early lesbian philosophers underscore the central role of the specular metaphor in the established discourses of Western science and epistemology. The very term theory (deriving from the Greek verb *theorein*, meaning 'to see') adequately reflects the ontological weight our culture traditionally attributes to the powers of vision. Paraphrasing the Russian philosopher Mikhail Bakhtin, we could say that, within the system of Western metaphysics, what can be known is that which can be seen.[6] And, perhaps even more pertinently, at least in the context of this book, the assumed connection between being and seeing alerts us to the crucial role of specularity in the Freudian account of sexuality, in which the perceivable absence/presence of a penis constitutes the mark of sexual difference, the founding structure of both subjective and objective reality.

These considerations substantially complicate the paradox of the subject at hand. If lesbian sexuality is not being 'countenanced' by the established conceptual order, how is it that such invisibility, or 'unknowability', can yet be argued to generate enhanced powers of vision with regard to the material and symbolic realities sustained by that order? What is more, if its ontological 'impossibility' renders lesbian sexuality culturally invisible, what could be the function of such a non-concept in the unconscious subtext underlying the collective imagination making up these realities? The purpose of this chapter is briefly to explore the paradoxical position of the lesbian in the symbolic universe of the contemporary West – a paradox, it will be clear, which centres on the notion of vision. By taking the pivotal epistemological notion of vision as a starting-point, I will argue that the 'impossible' lesbian subject's putative visionary powers are both cause and effect of her cultural invisibility – and *vice versa*. Directing my focus to a mode of discourse in which specularity figures centrally, that is, contemporary (Hollywood) cinema, I further hope to show that the specific cultural and theoretical configurations in which the lesbian has recently been gaining apparent visibility, in the final instance succeed in reinforcing the alarming subject's invisibility.

One might, however, at this point object that the question of the lesbian's cultural in/visibility has, in the years that have passed since radical feminist philosophers first heralded her advent in the role of visionary, become altogether obsolete. Has not this formerly unspeakable socio-sexual subject, in the course of the past decade, been more securely affirmed in her cultural presence than ever before in the history of the West? Have we not witnessed, since the latter half of the 1980s, an astounding growth in the production of popular films, primetime soaps and sitcoms featuring lesbians and lesbianism, as well as feature-length cover stories in a wide variety of mainstream journals and magazines, not to mention the host of scholarly books and fictional works by and about lesbians rolling off mainstream Anglo-American presses? And have not, more recently, Gay and Lesbian Studies been finding increasingly firm foothold in the Western academy? By way of beginning to answer at least some of these – not quite rhetorical – questions, I will, for the moment, restrict my focus to one representative yet controversial film which, partly as a result of its prominent media visibility, has provoked considerable debate in both Europe and the US, the Hollywood thriller *Basic Instinct* (1992), directed by the Dutch filmmaker Paul Verhoeven. Although a great deal already has been – and remains to be – said about the film as a whole, I will further limit my discussion to several striking scenes that appear particularly relevant to my argument.

Before I do so, however, let me point out that it is not my intention to show that *Basic Instinct* is, as a female art critic shortly after the film's release put it on BBC's *Late Show*, so obviously a male fantasy that it does not need to be taken seriously. Nor do I wish to suggest that the film should be banned or condemned because, as gay and lesbian activists in the US have protested, it exclusively features female characters whose unorthodox sexualities appear to be directly linked to, if not the actual result of, their equally 'perverse' criminal leanings. Yet, while most contemporary audiences probably realize that not *all* lesbians are psychopathic killers, I wonder if the majority of mainstream spectators indeed recognize the mythical Oedipal scenario of the film for what it is – an anxiety-ridden and violent male fantasy in which lesbianism plays a constitutive role. *Basic Instinct* therefore needs to be taken seriously precisely on account of the *less* obvious ways in which it reinscribes the founding narrative of phallocentric reality, that is, in Adrienne Rich's well-known phrase, the system of 'compulsory heterosexuality'. Or, as Lynda Hart has recently put it:

> *Basic Instinct* is a film worth the notice of feminist and lesbian theorists not because of its excessive rendering of the equation lesbian/man-hater – which is not much more than a banal repetition of male anxieties, fears, and fantasies – but because the film inadvertently makes evident the condensations and displacements that reproduce this link as a *structural* mechanism necessary to the power and pleasure of heteropatriarchy.[7]

Verhoeven's multimillion-dollar fantasy, then, especially requires critical analysis because of the paradoxical manner in which the almost monstrously disproportionate visibility of the 'lesbian' in this Hollywood blockbuster effectively succeeds in rendering lesbian sexuality all but invisible.

By referring to *Basic Instinct* as a male fantasy, the art critic on BBC's *Late Show* may or may not consciously have wished to draw attention to the unconscious subtext that subtends both heteropatriarchal power structures and most, if not all, Western malestream cultural production (to which *Basic Instinct* is no exception), that is, castration anxiety. The opening shots unmistakably reveal that this is the central motivating force of each of the film's various sub-plots, for the murder enacted in all its gory detail during the over-long scene represents the very scenario considered by Freud to constitute the inaugurating moment of (straight) male sexuality. The question, then, is not whether castration anxiety is central to the film, but rather what is its cause, and to whom/what is it directed? Is it the fantasy of 'the phallic mother', a figure originally invented by Freud and variously recreated by contemporary feminist and other theorists?[8] Is it the superior force of the maternal, the engulfing power of the womb that incites the ultimate existential *Angst* in the masculine imagination? Or, with a slightly different emphasis, is it the overwhelming 'riddle of femininity' that lies at the heart of the male's deepest ontological fears? Insofar as such fears can be seen to surface in Verhoeven's box-office hit, I would contend that, without excluding any of the above, their most significant source is formed by the spectral figure of the lesbian.

Basic Instinct opens with a series of slow-moving, almost surreal and fragmented images, that gradually turn into blurry shots of barely distinguishable body parts engaged in sexual intercourse. From our bird's-eye view on the fornicating couple's reflection in a wall-to-wall ceiling mirror, we are plunged headlong into the crevices of the masculine unconscious when the camera zooms in on a middle-aged man, helplessly lying on his back, his hands tied to the bedpost with a silk scarf, straddled by a blonde female skilfully riding the storm of his anxious pleasure. At the apparent *moment supréme*, the woman slyly reaches under the covers to produce an ice-pick with which she swiftly proceeds to furiously and repeatedly stab the prostrate male body. Whilst self-consciously inviting us to approach the film from a psychoanalytic perspective, the unexpectedness of the course of events, enhanced by a sudden break in the musical score, the lens-spattering blood, and the ruthlessness of the attack, all render this opening scene not just familiar, but also one of the most startlingly gruesome relays of the castration scenario I, for one, have ever seen.

Called to the scene of the crime is *Basic Instinct*'s nominal hero Nicky Curran, a.k.a. Shooter, a San Francisco-based detective played by the somewhat miscast star-actor Michael Douglas. Curran does not represent the stereotypically strong, unimpeachable defender of the law (familiar from detective movies of the 1940s and 1950s), but rather portrays the now equally stereotypical figure of the anti-hero, the tormented rebel/outcast who attained great popularity in 1960s' *film noir*. Suffering from repressed guilt about his wife's untimely death (she is reported to have committed suicide on account of his alcohol and drug abuse), Curran, it is further suggested, is traumatized by a shooting accident in which he killed two tourists who 'got into his firing line'. Tending to lose his temper and, it soon emerges, his sanity too, the jaded detective is evidently a liability within the police force, as a result of which he has been placed under compulsory psychiatric treatment.

In one of the first scenes we see Curran entering the office of his female therapist, Dr Beth Gardner, an attractive brunette with whom he has been having an affair only recently broken off – apparently because the doctor was unable to 'get it off' with her virile patient. While suggesting a reversal in terms of conventional gender relations – the detective literally depends on Gardner's professional authority to be declared fit for his job – the figure of the female 'shrink' would also seem the embodiment of the phallic mother. However, such formal female power, as well as the anxiety provoked by the potentially emasculating effects of the psychoanalytic probing into the male unconscious as such, are effectively neutralized by the fact that Gardner is shown still to desire her patient, while the latter has obviously lost sexual interest in her. Indeed, Curran points out that he would rather go without (venturing a bad joke about growing callouses on the inside of his hand) than engage in sexual activities with the unfulfilling female. Deftly exploiting this inequality in libidinal investment, he sets himself free from Gardner's psychic surveillance, and therewith procures authorization to proceed with his own professional investigations.

These investigations soon lead him to the film's most eye- and headline-catching character, Catherine Tramell (played by Sharon Stone), a figure undeniably adorned with several of the stereotypical trappings of the phallic mother, albeit in postmodern guise. At once fatally attractive, blatantly rich, and sexually (hyper)active, Tramell is presented as the best-selling author of juicy crime novels, whose horrifying plots all ominously appear to come true in the film's 'real' world. The powers of her beauty, and those she derives from her financial and sexual independence, are thus significantly strengthened by the fact that the glamorous creature, who holds degrees in both literature and psychology from UC Berkeley, is supposedly endowed with substantial intellectual and verbal powers as well. Nicky Curran is instantly enchanted by the irresistible *femme fatale*. His fearful fascination soon turns out to be a virtual obsession with death, for the moment the best-selling author decides to cast him as the main character of her next book, and to this purpose starts researching his past, she not only appropriates Curran's history, but also threatens to take over his character, portentously conveying that her psychological insights allow her accurately to predict his present as well as his future behaviour. Quite literally subjected to the uncanny visionary talents and presumed symbolic powers of his object of desire, the 'wacko' police officer seems all but delivered into Tramell's powerful hands.

Curran's apparent inferiority *vis-à-vis* his wealthy antagonist is enhanced by the fact that he is manifestly short of money. The resulting discrepancy in terms of economic power is not to be underestimated; this is, after all, the land of boundless opportunity. But Tramell is also the prime suspect in the case Curran is investigating, the appalling slaying of former rock 'n' roll star Johnny Bozz, which triggers off both the film's narrative and discursive movements. She thus additionally appears to be conversant with the narrative truth, a truth he seeks to discover. While the cunning female is suggested to possess the solution to the 'riddle' which governs the film on its surface level, the anti-heroic male, in contrast – though in line with generic conventions – begins his investigation with an utter lack of power/knowledge. He is, moreover, soon whisked out of the game altogether, for his superior officers (spurning Gardner's professional advice and thus further undercutting her putative authority), fear that the quick-tempered detective is not quite up to the job. Curran's symbolic disempowerment is therewith rendered 'official'. Yet, the quintessence of the castration anxiety as it is inscribed in this male fantasy is not located in any of the aforementioned features alluding to the fantasy of the phallic mother. By far the most daunting of Tramell's awesome characteristics, or so it appears, is her implied bisexuality. More precisely, the crux of Tramell's emasculating force does not seem to lie in her verbal, nor in her intellectual or financial, powers, but, instead, in her relationship with her female lover Roxy. It is on to this uncanny sexual Other, portrayed as a highly aggressive and obsessively jealous contender to the straight male's throne, that the existential terror provoked by the sinister suspect/object is consistently projected and hence displaced.

In an essay on the recent emergence of the 'lesbian serial killer' on the Western social scene, Camilla Griggers briefly comments on *Basic Instinct*, pointing to the widespread appearance of the lesbian 'double' in 1990s (Hollywood) cinema. Though actually a resurrection of a stock figure in Western folklore, the image of the lesbian as a woman who falls in love with her own mirror-image (an image that was reinforced and given 'scientific' grounding in the Freudian concept of the 'female homosexual's' perverse desire as the expression of a regressive narcissism), has become one of the tropes of lesbianism in twentieth-century cultural production.[9] Seen as a reworking of the traditional representation of the 'angry and vengeful woman – a woman who threatens to step beyond the bounds of heterosexual exchange', Griggers reads the character of Catherine Tramell as the embodiment of this 'screen woman', a cultural representation that is currently being '(dis)organiz[ed]' into 'two screen bodies, two clichéd images, which are two faces of the same fatal figure whose cold-blooded depredations threaten the nuclear family, the state police force, and heterosexual law and order'.[10] Whereas I depart from Griggers' otherwise persuasive reading of the movie insofar as she unquestioningly assumes Tramell to be the culprit of the string of violent crimes at the heart of its narrative tract, her analysis of the 'lesbian double' as a screen figure through which 'violence toward men and the nuclear family' can be channelled, and at the same time 'subject[ed] to both a narrative economy of violent retribution and a symbolic economy within the public sphere of ritual sacrifice' I consider particularly clarifying.[11] For it is, I will argue, precisely in her role of 'double' that the haunting figure of the lesbian underlines her function in *Basic Instinct*'s underlying castration scenario. The displacements effected by such doubling, however, instead of merely underscoring the 'female invert's' proverbial narcissism, at the same time mark Roxy's critical difference from her bisexual counterpart – the steamy sex scenes involving Tramell are, after all, exclusively heterosexual. That only the figure of the lesbian – and not just any trespassing or violent female – is capable of embodying the most fundamental threat to 'heterosexual law and order' becomes strikingly clear when we look more carefully at a number of scenes that lead up to the successful resolution of the film's heterosexual sub-plot.

One of these sequences forms a high point in terms of suspense, presenting an almost identical replay of the film's opening shots, this time offering us the voyeuristic pleasure of seeing Curran tied to the bedpost with a silk scarf, and Tramell straddling him. Needless to say, our anti-hero does not in the end suffer Bozz's distressing fate. Indeed, he is later to refer to the thrilling experience as the 'fuck of the century'. But to leave the value of such judgements aside, just as in the psychiatrist's office the sequence begins by ostensibly confusing traditional gender roles, placing Curran on the 'bottom' with a potentially psychopathic female 'on top'. The scene acquires special significance, however, when we learn that it is not only on the narrative stage that the film's underlying castration anxiety is overtly played out, but that it is, appropriately, in the frame's 'space-off' that the lesbian obliquely makes her critical presence felt in the Oedipal scenario here enacted.[12]

Although the camera focuses exclusively on the couple on the bed, we are retroactively led to infer Roxy's covert presence outside the frame of vision, for on several occasions we hear Tramell point out that her female companion enjoys watching her having sex with her male lovers. This psychosexual set-up signifies a reversal of conventional subject/object positions: the voyeuristic pleasure generally assumed to be the male prerogative is, in this instance, granted to a female subject, while the male hero is inserted into the narrative as the object of her gaze. On the face of it, such a configuration would appear to be a radical, if not subversive, narrative strategy. But is it? What is the lesbian allowed to see? Her ravishing lover having heterosexual intercourse with a run-down detective. What is more, as an audience, we do not perceive the pleasure Roxy is assumed to derive from watching; indeed, not only are we denied a view of the *voyeuse* herself, we are expected to share her pleasure, our look being aligned with the camera's close-up shots of the heady scene on the bed. A glimpse of the female pervert indulging in what generally counts as an exclusively male mode of pleasure – here presented as part of 'kinky' lesbian sexuality – is thus denied to us. The partiality of this vision of sexual pleasure and desire is entirely in line with the overall invisibility of the lesbian; insofar as lesbian sexuality has a place in Western culture, it is as a source, that is, *object* of voyeuristic titillation in mainstream (straight male) pornographical texts.

Whereas the herewith established triangulation of the characters' unorthodox sexual relationships at first glance seems to undercut the heterosexual gender system, the scene's follow-up shows that it does in effect constitute no more than a reinscription of a familiar scenario. For what the voyeuristic spectacle represents is, in psychoanalytic terms, the *Urszene* of the parental coitus, either actually observed or construed by the (boy) child; the so-called 'primal scene', which forms one of the *Urphantasien* (original fantasies) underlying the phallocentric imaginary. In his discussion of the primal scene, Freud infers that the observing (inevitably male) child perceives the act of heterosexual intercourse as an 'aggression by the father in a sado-masochistic relationship'. While giving rise to sexual excitation in the child, the scene is at the same time said to provide a 'basis for castration anxiety'. And, pointing up the repressed homosexual groundings of the fantasy, Freud further asserts that what is going on in the boy's field of vision is interpreted as 'anal coitus'.[13] In re-enacting one of the central fantasies underpinning our 'hom(m)osexual' culture,[14] *Basic Instinct* thus places the 'female invert' in the position of the male child. Lesbian sexuality is therewith assimilated to the dominant heterosexual paradigm, in that the operations of female same-sex desire are implied to mirror those of the straight male almost – but not quite – exactly. Shown to be no more than a copy of 'the real thing', the threat of sexual Otherness posed by the lesbian, consisting in her potentially destabilizing effect on normative power-gender relations, is kept at bay by the fact that the character is reduced to an 'aspiring' male.

These suppositions are confirmed by the conclusion of the sequence. It will be clear that, in order to assert his masculinity, Curran must insist on positioning Roxy in the role of his competitor; not, however, as the female lover of the woman he wants to possess for himself, but rather in the role most commonly assigned to the lesbian in heteropatriarchy, the man *manqué*. With the threat of lesbian Otherness thus being transformed into a copycat Sameness, she has become a familiar and recognizable rival to him.

The 'fuck of the century' having come to its climactic

conclusion, the sexual aftermath – Tramell peacefully asleep, Curran pensively smoking a cigarette – ends in the hero getting up from the bed and walking over to the bathroom to wash his face. While the camera first follows Curran's naked buttocks disappearing in the distance, the next shot zooms in to a close-up of his face, reflected in the bathroom mirror. Looking over his shoulder, we suddenly see the lesbian entering the frame from behind. The confused division of the narrative space, resulting from the indirect and mirroring camera angles, produces a sense of disorientation whose threat is enhanced by Curran's nakedness, which stands in sharp contrast to the black leather gear of his interlocutor. But despite the suggested vulnerability deriving from this disparity in protective covers, the hero's attitude is triumphant, self-assured, overbearing. His pleasure at this moment is evidently located in the fact that he has, so to speak, beaten the lesbian Other at what he imagines to be her Self/Same game, and is gloating over the conquest he has just made.

The suggested vulnerability of the exposed male body – already diminished by the fact that it is never fully exposed: we see Curran only from the waist up, the frame of the camera limiting our view to his torso while his (at the moment presumably rather flagging) genitals remain hidden from view – is swiftly annulled, when he turns around to confront his rival with a scornful look. Having redistributed the space by means of the power of his gaze, Curran further succeeds in placing his female opponent in the desired position by assuming an aggressive, discursive stance: 'Let me ask you something, Rocky, man to man. *I* think she is the fuck of the century, what do *you* think?' Both times I went to see *Basic Instinct* on the big movie screen, the audience around me, at this point, broke into loud and relieved laughter. Rather too excessive to be accounted for solely by Curran's not so original quip on his contestant's name, the source of such comic relief, it would appear, lies in the fact that, by thus renaming the lesbian, and (over)-masculinizing her desire, the hero enables himself to regain his male self-possession, while simultaneously exposing the futility of the inverted female's presumed masculine pretensions. The stereotypical image of the lesbian as an imitation of the straight male, lacking what we are not allowed to see, but which in its very absence proclaims its critical presence – that is, a penis

– is not only a familiar object of ridicule. It also serves as a powerful tool of realignment, whose effect cannot but be thoroughly reassuring. For what the scene invites us to infer is that Roxy, as an inferior copy of the genuine article, will ultimately be no match to any male hero – or anti-hero. And indeed, Curran's rivalry with his unsympathetic and, as it turns out, murderous opponent – a power contest emphatically set in motion by Curran himself – is satisfactorily concluded when, after a sensational wild chase through the streets of San Francisco, he succeeds in sending her car, and therewith his monstrous pursuer, to meet their final destination at the bottom of the bay.

But before we reach that triumphant victory, I want to go back for a moment to an earlier scene in which a similar kind of tension appears to be building up, that is, when an element of Otherness threatens to bring down the established system of power relations, only to be re-contained when the effect of such a threat seems to be most imminent. The sequence immediately precedes the sex scene discussed above and is set in a club (owned by the late Johnny Bozz), where Curran has followed the elusive object of his increasingly fervent desires. Donning an open V-neck sweater with nothing underneath, he appears vulnerable without his usual layers of professional male attire, a vulnerability which is underlined by the fact that the middle-aged, middle-class male is distinctly out of place amidst the fashionable pack of artsy-tartsy babyboomers freakishly dancing to the overwhelming beat of amplified house music. Curran's insecurity is palpable when he starts wandering through the flickering light looking for Tramell, but, not insignificantly, spotting Roxy first. Following the lesbian trail into – yes – the men's room, he finds himself confronted with what is evidently a nightmarish *tableau vivant*: Tramell sitting on a toilet seat framed by the doorpost, on one side seconded by her lesbian lover, on the other by a black (gay) male – in other words, by the most threatening forces of Otherness to male white heterosexual supremacy. Huddling over their cocaine, the three first send contemptuous looks up to the petrified Curran, after which Tramell extends one of her elegantly-stockinged legs to slam the door in his face. Thus excluded from the secretive triangle made up of the mysterious female, the lesbian, and the black gay male, the white male hero suffers extreme anxiety, a tension which we, the camera's look being aligned with Curran's throughout, are invited to experience vicariously.

The next shot returns us to the dance-floor, where Curran stands watching Tramell provocatively kissing Roxy. As on earlier occasions, these tantalizing 'lesbian' kisses serve as a titillating spectacle for the quasi-duped anti-hero: the erotic energy of the scene is not invested in either of the women, but rather aimed at the male watching them. Not long afterwards, Tramell abandons Roxy to the black male, and starts seducing Curran, the camera zooming in on her lower body rubbing his crotch, therewith directing attention away from the sexual and racial Others to the male Same, and the self-evident primacy of the (white) phallus. A visually rendered combat (in a series of shot-reverse-shots) between Curran and Roxy intercut the images of the former's swelling manhood. The scene not only conveys that the lesbian is destined to lose this power-contest, she is also shown to be a conspicuously bad loser: her behaviour signals anger, jealousy, and humiliation. In addition, the camera's focus on the sexual rivalry between the straight male and the lesbian pretender indicates that what is at stake is not so much the sexual object (Tramell) but rather the combative exchange itself. While the black man all but disappears into the background, the hero successfully appropriates the desired female object (which he keeps clasped in his arms throughout), but only after having subjected the *lesbian* to his power first. Since the remainder of the scene exclusively visualizes the consolidation of the newly-forged heterosexual bond, the passage first of all underlines the threat posed by female same-sex desire to male heterosexuality – or rather, to masculinity generally. It furthermore reveals that it is the defeat of the lesbian which forms the precondition of the conquest by which straight masculinity can and must be secured. And it finally also paves the way for Curran's eventual exoneration. When Roxy ends up dead as a direct result of their contest, her demise can be presented as clearly no fault of his: the self-assuming fake-male justly falls victim to her own lethal obsessions and murderous intentions.

In view of the ubiquitous presence of the lesbian in all these markedly heterosexualizing moments, I think one can safely say that it is not the enveloping force of femininity that invokes the male's castration anxiety as it obtains in this film's narrative and visual configurations: it is not Tramell's *vagina dentata* that poses the threat of obliteration to Curran's masculinity. On the contrary, it is in her potential *non*-availability that the desired object incites our hero's deepest fears. Being relegated to the margins of the detective plot is one thing, but the possibility of being excluded from the (hetero)sexual scenario is quite another. It is Tramell's sexual ambivalence that really lands the poor male in the throes of death agony. That Curran has officially been taken off the murder case underlines rather than challenges such a claim. On the one hand, his professional 'castration' clearly points to the definitive declaration of male redundancy that is, within the context of heteropatriarchy, represented by lesbian sexuality. On the other, the fact that he is able to pursue his investigations despite his lack of formal power to do so, indicates that the curtailing of his legal licence constitutes less of a hazard to the hero's masculinity than the sexual castration to which his disempowerment within the Law indisputably refers.

The successful elimination of scourge Roxy clears the way for Curran's ultimate survival. The film nonetheless insists on pointing out that our hero's escape has indeed been a narrow one, and primarily due to his phallic prowess. This is underlined by the fate suffered by Curran's kind-hearted buddy Gus. At an early point in the film, this amiable hill-billy reveals that he has 'not been getting any' for years, therewith establishing that he is no longer able to hold his 'masculine' own. Not surprisingly, it is the 'unmanly' male, not Curran, who is eventually brutally butchered to death by the ice-pick-wielding culprit of the film's initiating crime-plot, the hero's former lover/therapist, Dr Beth Gardner.[15] The female shrink, obviously taking her task (of cutting patients down to size) slightly too literally, is therewith exposed as the quintessential female monster, for it is at several points unequivocally suggested that the devouring impulses of the pretty brunette originate in her thoroughly disturbed and frustrated lesbian desires. Quite reassuringly, this pathological creature too is in the end efficiently exterminated by Curran.

Even the powerful Tramell, her transgressive phallic energies notwithstanding, eventually succumbs to the Law. Grieving over the loss of Roxy, she – somewhat implausibly – flings herself into the protective arms of the very man directly responsible for her companion's death. With the lesbian spectre, still shimmering through in the sole surviving female character, therewith also being erased, the hero seems to have successfully overcome the profound anxiety underlying the film's narrative tract as a whole. The ambivalence marking its ending, however, suggests that Curran does not win on all scores.

Bringing the narrative line full circle, the closing scene treats us to a final dose of voyeuristic pleasure. We witness Curran and Tramell lying in bed, talking about their future life together. But with the music ominously building up, the camera lowers its angle to zoom in on the glittering ice-pick under the bed, lying in wait, unseen by the unsuspecting hero. Allowing us a peek at the enduring presence of the castrating murder weapon, the text thus self-consciously intimates that the male subject's fear of emasculation cannot be eradicated by the killing off of individual lesbians: such terror is deeply entrenched within the masculine psychosystem. Underscored by a collective imagination in which lesbian sexuality is at once 'impossible' and, paradoxically, the condition upon which the myth of masculinity depends, it is precisely on account of its fantastic nature, as a product of male *Angst*, that the lesbian phoenix always threatens to rise again. The stereotypical image of the devouring lesbian vampire hence continues to be reborn, sustaining herself on the life-blood of those who envisage themselves her prospective victims.

Basic Instinct, while pretending to render the lesbian visible on the big slick Hollywood screen, in the final analysis thus confirms the continuing prevalence of a cultural scheme delineated almost twenty years ago by the lesbian philosophers cited earlier in this chapter. What the film depicts is a reality in which the 'lesbian' can only be, and be seen as, a bad copy of the straight male; a conceptual universe, moreover, from which she also, paradoxically, must be violently erased. Indeed, although the alarming subject is, as I hope to have shown, of central significance to each of the film's various sub-plots, the actual word 'lesbian' is not uttered once during its almost two-hour run.

In her quite literal discursive absence from Western culture, the lesbian subject continues to occupy a position which not only differs radically from that of straight male and female subjects, but also from that of gay males. As Judith Butler has persuasively argued, within Western societies the male homosexual serves as the exception to confirm the rule, occupying a discursive space as 'prohibited object' within the terms of the heterosexual contract, in relation to which the law of Nature can reassert itself. Whereas 'homosexualities of all kinds ... are being erased, reduced, and (then) reconstituted as sites of radical homophobic fantasy,' it is, she maintains, precisely as outlawed objects that male homosexualities are in effect perpetually (re)constituted by official as well as reverse-discourses within society's dominant 'grids of cultural intelligibility'. Lesbians, in contrast, are 'not even named nor prohibited within the economy of the law'.[16] The mandatory falsification of lesbianism in Western socio-cultural schemes hence shows that it is not compulsory heterosexuality *per se*, but compulsory *female* heterosexuality, which is the condition upon which the 'natural' order of things or, to be more precise, of the founding social contract, depends.[17] Only by being relegated to, in Butler's words, a 'domain of unthinkability and unnameability' can the lesbian be culturally present: as an 'abiding falsehood', as a 'copy, an imitation, a derivative example, a shadow of the real'. It is as a site of negativity or discursive absence (effectively reinscribed by terms like 'female homosexual') that the category 'lesbian' can and must function as the 'abject' of the cultural consciousness.[18]

The question remains, however, what exactly determines the lesbian's presumed 'uniqueness' that would necessitate such exclusion from the symbolic order, and perpetually condemn her to a site of negativity, to a function at the culture's abjected under-side. Butler proposes that the lesbian, by conspicuously performing the 'unthinkable', embodies a threat of exposure to both gay and straight upholders of the law, since her alleged sexual 'mimicry' represents exactly the kind of drag which 'enacts the very structure of impersonation by which *any gender* is assumed.' The 'monstrous' creature thus would not only confuse the proper functioning of the heterosexual order, but also threaten to subvert the 'ontologically consolidated phantasms of "man" and "woman"'.[19] In order to ensure the self-presence of heterosexual women and straight as well as gay men in their identities as genuine and authentic 'male' and 'female' subjects, the lesbian's 'abnormality' must consequently be set off as an imitation against the real thing: 'natural' heterosexuality, which, as we have seen is, in an economy of the Same, in fact the term of 'hom(m)osexuality'. My brief analysis of *Basic Instinct* would appear sufficiently to support this line of argument.

In what is so obviously a male fantasy, Verhoeven's film constitutes a precise and anguished re-enactment of the compulsory cultural play which serves to secure the 'realness' and stability of categories like 'man' and 'woman'. In this respect, I find myself in complete agreement with the BBC-spokesperson cited earlier. What this evidently *gender*-conscious female art critic failed to point out, however, and what may indeed be far less obvious to mainstream movie audiences, is that the film also explicitly articulates the pervasive lesbophobic drive that underlies the conceptual system in/through which the binary and oppositional categories of heterosexual gender are both enacted and produced.

In what is, then, to all intents and purposes, a specifically *lesbo-* (as distinct from homo-)phobic cultural context, the putative visionary powers of the 'unthinkable' lesbian subject hence both reside in and derive from the fact that her 'gaze of inversion', when critically directed at the founding conceptual schemes of Western civilization, threatens to disrupt the abject subtext underlying the narrative of its history as a whole. The overdetermined quality of the violence with which popular films such as *Basic Instinct* seek to screen out and eradicate the lesbian spectre from the field of vision, indicates that such a proposition is perhaps not so exaggerated as it may seem. Nor is the expression of lesbophobic violence the sole privilege of the notoriously violent and phobic productions of the Hollywood dream machine. As we shall see in a moment, the 'monstrous' figure of the lesbian may equally be evoked – only to be abjected from – the supposedly more 'sophisticated' contemporary European movie screen.

3 Impossible Subject among Multiple Cross-overs: Roman Polanski's *Bitter Moon*

> The disclosure of a homosexual identity produces such intense fantasies of destruction because the knowledge that is imparted impacts on the subjects to whom the information is directed. That is, it is not simply a disclosure of one's 'self' that the homosexual coming out effects, but also always a shattering of the recipient's fantasy of a stable sexual identity.
>
> Laura Hart, *Fatal Women*

In these 'multicultural' times, gender, ethnicity, race and class enjoy widespread recognition as significant categories in the construction of both private and public meanings. In current theoretical practice, among the most 'urgent' questions appear to be those centring on (inter)ethnicity, postcolonialism, indeed, on whatever can be subsumed under the overall heading of 'multiculturalism'. And whereas the concept itself continues to provoke extensive debate among cultural critics and social theorists alike – ranging from celebratory embraces of multiple 'pluralisms', to laments about the loss of distinctive privileges – such reactions nonetheless signify that the blurring of ethnic/racial boundaries is increasingly being recognized as an irreversible aspect of life in the contemporary West.[1]

Developments in popular culture indicate that the crossing of gender boundaries is also becoming gradually accepted, not just by the select few, but in Western society at large. The overwhelming success of gender-bending performers like Madonna, Prince and Michael Jackson shows that a deliberate destabilization of traditional gender lines is no longer restricted to the realm of the (sub)cultural avant-garde. Still, while in the transgressive acts of these megastars both forms of boundary-crossing are often effectively intertwined, the hyped-up scandal about Michael Jackson's alleged (homo)sexual escapades reveals that there are still boundaries that may not so easily be crossed. Like Bill Clinton's ongoing struggles over the issue of homosexuality in the US military, the media coverage of what first appeared an almost unplumbable source of profit (but soon turned into a virtual non-event by Jackson's post-haste marriage to Lisa Marie Presley) suggests that, even though some of the major social structures are thoroughly in flux, there are yet demarcation lines that will not be smoothly eradicated: the crossing of sexual borders can still be cause of substantial public outrage. Tying in with an ardent defence of heterosexual marriage and the nuclear family as the ultimate safeguards against the loss of 'traditional values', sexual 'normality' appears to figure as one of the last remaining strongholds of a former Moral Majority – currently gaining renewed and widespread support as the New Right – in an otherwise thoroughly destabilized, differentiated, postmodern culture.

In the light of these and other recent outbursts of rampant homophobia, it is all the more remarkable that lesbian sexuality – historically, we have seen, one of the most invisible cross-over figures confined to the shadowy regions of the cultural imagination – has, over the past few years, been enjoying steadily growing, indeed unprecedented, media visibility. Since the early 1990s mainstream magazines such as *Harpers & Queen*, *Newsweek*, *US News*, *Elle* and *Vanity Fair* have been virtually competing with one another in turning out the most outrageous or shocking cover stories on famous 'real life' lesbians. Furthermore, the figure of the lesbian outlaw has begun to appear covertly, yet unmistakably, in ostensibly straight films such as *Thelma and Louise* (1991), and, in a much more outspokenly lesbophobic way, in *Single White Female* (1992) and *The Hand that Rocks the Cradle* (1992).[2] An enormously successful, popular film like *Basic Instinct* (1992) can, I have suggested, actually afford to proudly present openly 'lesbian' characters, without losing any of its power to attract mass audiences around the globe. The more sedate world of the most domesticized of media channels, television, has also

become a venue for varied, somewhat less conspicuous representations of female 'perversion'. Around the same time that (persistently violent, usually murderous) Hollywood 'lesbians' began
drawing a great deal of public attention, the impossible subject
also made her appearance in our living rooms, featuring in such
highly-praised, prestigious BBC productions as *Portrait of a
Marriage* (1992) (based on Harold Nicholson's memories of his
mother, Vita Sackville-West, and the latter's passionate love-
affair with Violet Trefusis), and the four-part mini-series *Oranges
Are Not the Only Fruit* (1991), adapted from Jeanette Winterson's
novel of the same title. Somewhat more fleetingly, lesbian figures
additionally made their débuts in evening soaps such as, notoriously, *LA Law*. Whilst featuring prominently in the most celebrated American sitcom of the early 1990s, *Roseanne*, lesbian
characters repeatedly made cameo appearances in cop shows like
NYPD Blue and *Law & Order*. The upmarket trend in popular
lesbian iconography has not left the academic publishing market
unaffected, as is clear from the recent outpouring of book
releases on what is obviously not only a fashionable but also a
profitable popular subject.[3] In short, in our postmodern, multi-
media culture, lesbianism has not only become quite glaringly
visible, but also an exciting new trend, a kinky 'new lifestyle',
palatable to even the most mainstream of mainstream audiences.

Emerging under the various signs of the 'new lesbian' (I have
never been able to find out what exactly the 'old' *popular* lesbian
looked like), a.k.a. the 'lipstick lesbian' or, alternatively, the
'designer dyke', this newly discovered figure of psychosexual
Otherness is not only, as Cathy Griggers astutely remarks, 'going
broadcast' and 'going technoculture', she is also 'going mainstream'.[4] The point is not a minor one. For however subversive
the very emergence of the 'new lesbian' may seem, the ostensibly
transgressive figures crowding the stage in recent, upscale popular
cultural production usually tell a somewhat different story than it
would first appear. Being assimilated into the mainstream, the
postmodern lesbian's extravaganzas, in effect, more often than
not merely present a thrilling sexual spectacle, or titillating inter-
lude (what else is new?) in a still pervasively heterocentrist cultural scenario. Becoming commercially viable as an eccentric
'new lifestyle', lesbian sexuality, as it is predominantly presented

in the media today, largely evolves into no more than a trendy option, a potentially profitable commodity. What the current upsurge in popular 'lesbian' images hence primarily conveys is that lesbianism no longer constitutes a reliable ground for subcultural formation, nor a potential source of either personal or collective empowerment. That is to say, the commodification of lesbianism would seem effectively to put paid to what used to be the primary goals of gay and lesbian liberation movements: social organization and radical political action. Having little to do with lesbianism as either a structural aspect of psychosexual or self-defined social identity, the 'new lesbian lifestyle' would hence seem to render any concept of a 'politics of (sexual) identity', as a mobilizing force in a political movement aimed at social change, essentially obsolete.

Griggers, in the essay referred to above, rightly emphasizes that the question of 'identity' never arises out of nowhere, but is, in fact 'always a problem of signification in regard to historically specific social relations'.[5] In other words, the relations between the processes of signification, particularly those operative in cultural production, and the socio-political power structures in which any mode of meaning-production obtains, are of a profoundly intertextual nature. Being tightly bound up with shifting but historically specific social relations, all cultural expression is therefore at once inescapably interested and socio-politically overdetermined. This holds especially true when questions of sex, sexuality and gender are concerned. Since no cultural phenomenon occurs in a void, the lesbian's rapid rise from impossible subject to cultural commodity cannot be considered accidental, nor even the unexpected product of the perverted brains of a few eager-for-profit media moguls. The glamorous (re)birth of this former psychosexual outcast should, I suggest, be critically examined in the light of a socio-cultural climate in which growing divisions among and within dominant and non-dominant groups alike seem to forestall the possibility of political organization based on a shared sense of identity; a social context, moreover, in which an ostensible focus on multiculturalism serves as a smoke-screen to cover up the ever-deepening rifts in the texture of Western societies generally.

In order to trace the current commodification of lesbian sexuality back to its origins in the larger (multi)cultural formation – or, as some would prefer, in the age of postmodernity – it is necessary to explore the meanings of recent popular inscriptions of lesbianism, as much as their underlying suppositions, and perhaps even more so when these surface in relation to other forms of socio-cultural differentiation. It strikes me that mainstream representations of female same-sex desire are almost without exception framed against and eventually subsumed by the operations of modes of cultural differentiation other than sexual ones. Ethnic, racial or class issues frequently appear to have been the focus of attention after all, while shifting definitions of gender tend to provide both the starting-point and the cast within which the lesbian's border-crossings are ultimately contained. Roman Polanski's captivating film *Bitter Moon* (1992) is a case in point. While certainly not representative of malestream film production as a whole (heavily burdened, as his work usually is, with the imprint of the director's highly idiosyncratic psychosexual obsessions), *Bitter Moon* nonetheless constitutes a representative example of the deceptive ways in which the cultural mainstream appropriates lesbian sexuality for its own purposes. It furthermore allows us to trace the significance of the elusive cross-over figure as the embodiment of psychosexual otherness that often comes to carry the weight of a whole range of other modes of difference; 'othernesses' that, each in their own way, have increasingly come to jeopardize white, straight male socio-cultural supremacy.

A French/British production launched in Europe some two years prior to its more recent release in the US, *Bitter Moon* is very much a narrative film. It addresses various modes of cultural differentiation, most prominently the aspects of gender and sexuality. The film is not, however, a narrative *about* any particular category of difference. Rather, the processes of socio-cultural *différance* the film engages are conjoined with the similar processes of discourse in such a way that all forms of identity, instead of being rendered in narrative form, are shown to *be*, essentially, nothing but stories. Since it is obviously the act of story-telling, as distinct from the story itself, which informs *Bitter Moon*'s narrative dynamic, one might, in fact, go so far as to say that Polanski's engrossing fantasy self-consciously points up that narrative and narration jointly enact the ongoing 'reality' of human subjectivity.

Calling into question established notions of gendered identity in relation to both sexuality, race, class, age and nationality, *Bitter Moon* presents itself (by means of the male voice-over) as an articulation of the intertwining operations of symbolic and sexual power. In its insistence on its own discursivity, the film underlines the fact that the conceptual framework which sustains our phallo-, ethno- and heterocentric social order derives its compelling force from being nothing but a fiction, a many-layered and never-ending story. Such explicit recognition of the delusive quality of its subtending ideologies, or cultural myths, and therewith of the precarious nature of prevailing socio-cultural power structures themselves, will, I suspect, no longer come as a surprise to even a mainstream contemporary audience. That both the tenacity and the ultimate unsustainability of these myths, in particular the film's underlying Oedipal plot, are explicitly linked to an hitherto largely invisible sexual scenario is nonetheless remarkable. Whilst showing up the brittle foundations of Eurocentric heteropatriarchy by deliberately poking fun at the myth of white masculinity, and by furthermore throwing into overall confusion the dominant system of power-gender relations, what the film's narrative tract eventually chokes on is lesbian sexuality. Lesbian sexuality functions as at once the indigestible and indispensable plot-space in this male fantasy, simultaneously its *sine qua non* and its vanishing-point. In the following exploration of the critical function of the lesbian in Polanski's revamped Oedipus myth, I will attempt to elucidate how and why this specific mode of boundary-crossing cannot but operate as an ultimately inassimilable configuration in an otherwise highly self-reflexive, if not parodic, narrative enactment of a fundamentally destabilized white hetero-masculinity.

Bitter Moon is set up as a frame story. Its primary narrative line unfolds on board a European cruise ship headed for Istanbul and eventually, Bombay. The idea of travel as a liberating experience is enhanced by the opening shot, which directs our gaze through a porthole to take in an ever-expanding view of the open sea. Suggesting the possibility of cutting loose from one's moorings, of a temporary transcendence of the bounds of history and geography, the sequence projects an enabling timespace in which national and cultural borders may smoothly, almost naturally be crossed. The ostensibly liberatory atmosphere, however, swiftly proves to be quite deceptive. It is, in fact, precisely in its sequestration from the 'real world' that the story's closed temporal and spatial setting is shown to entail the necessity of self-definition, of demarcating the Self as distinct from Others, in highly polarizing, even oppositional terms. All of the characters momentarily suspended in this virtual no man's land are driven by a need to impose their individuality on these uncharted grounds, taking great pains to culturally 'frame' themselves by setting off their distinct national identities against those of the various, here provisionally assembled, Others.

The fact that the ship is sailing from the West to the East immediately acquires pointed significance when we meet the film's nominal protagonists, Nigel and Fiona Dobson (played by Hugh Grant and Kristin Scott Thomas). This very British, upper-middle-class couple, it transpires, are sailing to the magical Orient in order to bring some life back into their seven-year, evidently somewhat stale, marriage. Their encounter with the Indian widower Mr Singh (played by Victor Banerjee) and his five-year-old daughter Amrita results in the first cross-cultural confrontation.

Abiding by the rules of his rigorous public-school education, well-groomed 'thirtysomething' Nigel embarks on polite conversation, expressing his supposedly postcolonially-correct view of India as a mythical realm that has 'so much to teach the West'. The embodiment of jingoist English bigotry, the effete young Briton is at once put in his place by the light-hearted Mr Singh, who cheerfully dismisses such lofty views of his native country as the 'karma-nirwana-syndrome' commonly shared by its former colonizers. But when Mr Singh, at a later point, offsets his own down-to-earth image of India by depicting an equally exotic England in terms of pastoral fields and lush green pastures, we are forced to realize that both ex-colonizer and ex-colonized are dramatizing their sense of individual identity by articulating the most threadbare clichés about each other's national origins and cultural horizons. With the two male characters staking out their symbolic territory by enlarging the gap between their contrasting socio-historical positions, the woman figuring in this scene meanwhile assumes her appropriate gender role by emphatically staying out of the 'portentous' conversation, in order to concentrate her attention instead on the motherless girl obediently standing by. When Mr Singh subsequently volunteers that 'children are a better form of marriage therapy than any trip to India', the increasingly palpable racial/cultural tension marking the scene is displaced by the invocation of heterosexual reproduction as a universally valid recuperative phenomenon. Not only does 'providing for [one's] posterity' appear to be the best way to overcome marital problems, and thus to smooth out relations between the sexes, it is also presented as a panacea whose healing powers serve to transcend and reconcile postcolonial (male) power relations. With the restoration of a clearly transcultural hom(m)osexual bond, the impending culture clash between the ethnically distinct Self/Same males is thus effectively defused, while the imposition of the heterosexual imperative simultaneously sets up the female Other as a mediating (maternal) space in the service of a 'globalized' Mankind.

Such a reconciliatory procedure, whereby a potential socio-cultural clash as a result of one mode of difference is deferred by the installation of another, informs each of the several story-lines along which the film's intricate narrative pattern unfolds. It is, in effect, this very plot mechanism which allows for the various story-lines eventually to intersect, and to bring the film as a whole to its final resolution.

Bitter Moon's framing plot is set in motion when the inane British couple inadvertently become involved with a middle-aged American invalid by the name of Oscar Benton (played by Peter Coyote), and his young French wife Mimi (Emmanuelle Seigner). The 'obnoxious cripple' soon not only comes to dominate the film's main story, but also succeeds in drawing both audience and characters into a spellbinding tale of passion, sex, and ultimately, violence. By taking up his part as the narrator/protagonist on a subordinate level of narration, Oscar shows that the power of the word does not reside in just any type of discourse: it is the practice of story-telling which allows the otherwise quite literally disempowered male to assume his socio-symbolic power over the microcosmic world aboard the ship, and, in the same move, to take control of the projected reality on the movie screen.

When Nigel is buttonholed by the uncanny American, he has

already lost his proverbial British decency by developing a not so decent desire for the latter's irresistible wife. Promised that he can 'have' the 'stunning' creature on condition that he first hears Oscar out, he allows himself to be lured by the 'obscene' *raconteur*'s bewitching verbal powers – who, incidentally, explains his unusual generosity by pointing out that he 'rather supervise[s] [his wife's] affairs than submitting to them'. The focus of Oscar's enchanting yarns is, not surprisingly, the object of Nigel's illegitimate desires. It does not take long, however, for the priggish young man to become obsessed not just with the story's highly charged object, but also with the narrating subject himself.

Cashing in on familiar stereotypes, *Bitter Moon* insists throughout on foregrounding discrepancies in sexual mores and morality by explicitly relating these to the characters' diverse national backgrounds. Characterized by Oscar as an 'English rose' and a 'walking mantrap' respectively, prim Fiona and luscious Mimi are defined in their disparate sexual identities by their physical appearance as much as by their contrasting British and French accents. What Nigel describes as Oscar's 'verbal exhibitionism' further stands in such striking contrast to his own stilted upper-class lingo, that the difference in the two males' sexual temperaments is expressly located in their disparate discursive styles. But although the film derives much of its momentum from highlighting such sexual-cultural dissimilarities, the two men gradually become united in their narrative quest for one and the same object: the fantasy called Woman – a story whose cross-cultural, indeed, mythical significance is underscored by the (fairy-tale-like) opening line with which Oscar succeeds in first engaging his captive audience: 'Eternity began for me one fine afternoon in Paris'.

In a series of lengthy flashbacks we learn that the American invalid, once a would-be writer, has at an early age left his native country to settle in his 'dream city' Paris, eager to follow in the footsteps of his famous fellow-countrymen Hemingway, Miller, and Scott Fitzgerald, pictures of whom line the walls of his stylish Left Bank apartment. Frankly acknowledging that he himself presents a rather pale reflection of his idealized heroes, the expatriate artist was, at the time, evidently satisfied with living off his predecessors' dreams: we retrospectively witness him living the promiscuous life of the expatriate bohemian artist to the hilt. Whilst providing the historical background to the story unfolding on the surface level, these reminiscences also suggest that the process of Oscar's discursive self-construction, in the past as well as the film's narrative present, is pervasively animated by his legendary role-models' masculine spirits. And, though a (self-acknowledged) failure as a writer, it is Oscar's talent for self-aggrandizing fantasy that tempts the unimaginative Nigel into his 'sordid' male orbit. Both Oscar's riveting story, that is, the story-within-the-story, and *Bitter Moon*'s framing narrative, thus critically turn on the power of the imagination.

His overstated squeamishness notwithstanding, we see Nigel compulsively returning to Oscar's lower-deck hut, allowing himself to be lured into a space even more secluded from the 'real world' than the confined social realm aboveboard. Swayed by his progressively feverish desires, he yearns to learn more about their object, Mimi, in whom his beguiling host once believed to have found 'all the beauty of the world embodied in one perfect female form.' Having witnessed the American expatriate meet his fate in the form of a young French dance student on a Parisian bus, we too become engrossed in the passionate story that issues from this first romantic encounter.

Further flashbacks show us the couple, despite obvious differences in age, nationality, and social positions, embarking on what appears to be a perfect love affair. A series of sunny, happy scenes show them paying ample tribute to the French capital's legendary status as the 'city of love'. The greater part of Oscar's reminiscences, however, is taken up by their swiftly developing, not so traditional sex life. Dexterously handling a variety of suitably bizarre paraphernalia, they are depicted (in great and graphic detail) enacting the most unorthodox sexual scenarios, until their unbridled fantasies begin to lose their mesmerizing power. With the sexual excitement beginning to wear off, Oscar at once loses interest in his playmate altogether. Mimi, in contrast, though evidently well-versed in the discourse of desire, is young enough still to believe in the myth of romance. When Oscar brusquely shatters such domesticating dreams and sends his former dominatrix packing, Mimi rapidly turns from a sensual 'sorceress' into a pathetic supplicant, desperate to ensnare her prize 'Tiger' in her connubial nets. Determined to rid himself of the clinging creature, the latter devises and implements an impressive range of increasingly sadistic humiliations. When he finally believes that he has delivered himself from her smothering female clutches, however, Mimi returns on the narrative stage to assume the guise of a genuine nemesis. In an agonizing scene, she flips Oscar out of the hospital bed in which he is recuperating from a car accident, therewith irrevocably destroying his already multi-fractured legs.

Having quite literally castrated him – the philanderer's once so active sexual organ is just as permanently paralysed as the rest of his lifeless lower body – Mimi subsequently turns into the person-ification of the phallic mother. Assuming the role of resident nurse, she takes complete control of Oscar's life, and, showing herself at least as inventive as her prey, subjects him to the most awful humiliations. Rejecting her role as repudiated female, Mimi successfully tips the scales in the sexual power-struggle: not, how-ever, to abandon the invalid to his miserable fate, but rather to become his lifelong tormentor. Although the one-time Don Juan is in his turn exposed to the most excruciating forms of psycho-sexual torture, he appears to accept his subaltern position with remarkable resignation. Indeed, watching Oscar visibly relishing his bitter accounts of the cataclysmic passion that binds him and the implacable goddess of vengeance together, we are led to infer that he derives considerable pleasure from his subjection to Mimi's sadistic fantasies. Significantly, this bond is lastingly forged when the omnipotent chaperone one night treats her cap-tive audience to an extended seduction scene, eventually getting it off with an athletic black dancer in front of Oscar's anguished eyes. Marking the 'rubicon' of passion and cruelty, this cross-racial sexual spectacle, Oscar later recounts, would prove the 'catharsis' that landed them, like 'survivors of a catastrophe', on a plateau 'shared by no one else in the world'.

However physically disempowered he may be, the impotent hero's existence is thus, like a postmodern Rochester's, fully legit-imated by his key role as the broken anti-hero of Mimi's vindic-tive scenario. Indeed, not only is Oscar the central character in the (female) plot of retribution: as the film's narrator on its inter-connecting plot-levels, he has thus far also retained his power as the subject of (his own) discourse. Since the male's superior symbolic position has remained factually unchallenged, the film's Oedipal plot has been able to unfold uninterrupted. It is only when Mimi breaks with the conventions of (Oedipal) narrative *per se*, that the intertwining story-lines inevitably come to their startlingly violent mutual endings.

Bitter Moon reaches its climax when, marking the moment of narrative intersection, its female object escapes the male subject's socio-symbolic and narrative supervision: defying Oscar's promise to Nigel, Mimi decides to have sex with the latter's wife instead. She therewith not only breaks the seemingly fireproof heterosexual bond between Oscar and herself, but also undermines the newly (re)inscribed hom(m)osexual alliance between the two men. Unlike the extended coverage of earlier sexual frolics, the sinister lesbian tryst significantly takes place outside the camera's, and thus our own, field of vision. Its foreplay, a protracted sequence on the dance floor (amidst an upper-middle-class crowd going wild), is unmistakably presented as an enticing spectacle to its various groups of spectators: both women's slightly bewildered husbands, their fellow passengers, and ourselves, the movie audience. Having resulted in a somewhat clumsily exchanged kiss (though barely visible, this revolting act causes one of the partying elderly ladies to throw up into her paper hat), the scene of perversion is prematurely concluded when the interlocking female shapes walk out of the picture together.

After a brief intervening shot of a defeated Nigel making his way to his cabin to finish a solitary bottle of whisky, we return to the lower deck, where Oscar sits watching the two naked 'nymphs' sleeping off their implied 'amatory exertions'. Both the visual eclipse of the lesbian sex scene itself and the figurative terms in which it is cast – Oscar, never at a loss for a flowery expression, describes the unspeakable event as an 'allegory of grace and beauty' – render the masked lesbian moment into an elusive metaphor, underscoring its function as the vanishing-point of the film's Oedipal narrative as a whole. By pulling out of the heterosexual plot, Mimi, the female Other on which the narrator's fragmented Self depends, has broken the most fundamental of phallocentric laws. Both her own role and that of the story's male subject are herewith conclusively played out. In a last, desperate attempt at reasserting his claim to symbolic power, Oscar uses a gun – phallic substitute *par excellence* – to end the story. To Nigel's shock and horror, he puts a bullet through his head – making sure, however, to shoot the female transgressor first. This brutal assassination confirms that the hero's exclusion from the antagonizing 'lesbian' scene signifies his ultimate emasculation. By killing the treacherous female, the ousted male, while ostensibly maintaining control over narrative events, in effect underscores his actual effacement from the 'invisible' lesbian moment, a virtual non-moment that at once constitutes the narrative's turning-point and reveals the film's underlying core of castration anxiety.

Polanski's cleverly composed nightmare shows that, among the various threats of Otherness it brings to bear on the male protagonists, it is not the fantasy of the predatory black male, nor that of the phallic mother which marks the end of white straight masculinity. Oscar's phallic competence may have been challenged by one and literally annihilated by the other; it is, in the end, the threat of lesbian Otherness that heralds the irreversible obliteration of his male Self. Conspicuously veiled, the pivotal cross-over moment, however, has little to do with lesbian sexuality *per se*, that is, as an active mode of female sexuality autonomous from men. No such thing can be allowed to exist, or even be recognized within the terms of the film's defining narrative contract. Mimi's wandering from the straight path consequently results in instant execution, whereas Fiona (obviously rather taken aback by the unexpected turn of events) is resolutely restored to her stuffy British husband. The fleeting female same-sex desire that plays such a crucial part in the development of the film's intertwining plots is thus at once presented as an 'unenvisageable' male fantasy, and reduced to a subordinate factor in the film's Oedipal underpinnings. Bringing the narrative line full circle, the closing scene zooms in on Nigel and Fiona seeking comfort in each other's arms, while little Amrita Singh, dutifully assuming her prospective mediating role, comes over to offer them her father's best wishes.

Rendered invisible, indeed, 'unthinkable' within the terms of the symbolic Law, being inconceivable within dominant grids of cultural intelligibility, lesbianism belongs, to recall Butler's argument, to the unconscious *abject* of the Western imagination.[6] That the figure of the lesbian causes inordinate cultural anxiety, is, I think, adequately conveyed by the metaphysical overkill with which a typical Hollywood production, such as *Basic Instinct*, but also a much more complex film like *Bitter Moon*, which at first sight appears to offer a more subtle and self-reflexive account of embattled white masculinity, insist on removing the 'impossible' subject from view. Already having reduced lesbian sexuality to a function in their variously re-enacted Oedipal plots, both films additionally express a compelling need to violently obliterate the unnameable *abject* from their discourse altogether.

In seeking to control lesbian Otherness, malestream culture in general tends to insert lesbian images into the very master narratives that keep heteropatriarchy going. This is not exactly a new phenomenon; in fact, the incorporation of lesbian moments, trysts, and spectral appearances in otherwise exclusionary heterosexual scenarios has, we have seen in earlier chapters, been part of the Western cultural tradition for many centuries.[7] Even so, whereas the lesbian's haunting presence hardly ever amounts to more than a suggestive hovering at the edges of the mainstream cultural imaginary, the lesbian ghost emerges ubiquitously, and in the most unlikely places, at the very moment when traditional social structures are under attack, or when dominant systems of power/knowledge are, in effect, being shaken to their foundations. In the more recent past, such upsurges of lesbian imagery could generally be directly linked to the changing position of women in society; in other words, explained as part of an anxious response to the undermining effects on hegemonic power structures brought about by any increase in female socio-economic and symbolic agency. In the post-war period, for instance, when women who had been working outside the home in previous years (to replace a shrinking male work-force) refused to be sent back into the kitchen once their men returned from the front, a number of mainstream films, not to mention a whole range of cheap paperback novels, featured or, indeed, concentrated on 'unnatural passions' among women. Needless to say, these unnatural figures, who were shown to wreak great havoc by leading 'normal' innocent women astray and therewith threatening to bring the social process as such to a halt, were almost without exception eventually subjected to some sort of terrible punishment, frequently ending up dead. (As a rule, such diabolical figures are killed by a noble male hero, who thus not only conquers the corrupting force of perversion, but additionally procures the temporarily lapsed woman for himself.)

Despite her more glamorous outlook and wider range of cultural venues, the postmodern figure of the 'lipstick lesbian', as she currently emerges in the mainstream of contemporary cultural production and in the mass media generally, impresses me as not all that different from her monstrous predecessors. Nor does it seem particularly surprising that it is at this specific socio-historical juncture, when all sorts of boundaries – be it national, geographic, socio-cultural, gender, ethnic or racial – are in the process of becoming blurred and destabilized, that the ghostly lesbian once again figures prominently on the cultural scene. What does surprise and occasionally disturb me, is that the 'gorgeous' looks of the contemporary 'designer dyke' (we should not forget that *attractive* lesbians were up till now practically unheard of, the idea of physical beauty and female same-sex desire being virtually oxymoronic in patriarchal folklore), appears to have a somewhat blinding effect on even the more critical consumers of popular cultural imagery.[8] Seen by some as signs of a triumphant rebirth, the majority of the ravishing lesbian beauties presently populating the (overwhelmingly male-dominated) mainstream cultural domain are, after all, still inserted into our field of vision in blatantly lesbophobic ways; that is to say, as at once irresistible lures and as highly powerful threats of destruction, which not only require, but quite obviously justify commodification and containment, if not violent obliteration.

An explicit example of this procedure appeared a few years ago in a special summer issue of the Dutch edition of the international *Avant Garde*. Picking up on a trend set earlier by magazines like *Newsweek, US News* and *Vanity Fair*, this highly popular glossy evidently saw profit in appealing to its supposedly cosmopolitan audience with a titillating item on female same-sex desire. Led on by the tempting headline, 'Getting the Hots for Your Girlfriend', we learn that lesbianism, according to the female author, is not a potential form of cultural identity, nor even a private 'preference', but indeed, an excitingly 'new lifestyle'.[9] Thrilling reports on the emergence of the 'lipstick lesbian' among the pleasure-seeking smart sets of London and Los Angeles hence issue in what would otherwise have been a remarkable inference, i.e., that it has 'suddenly become fashionable to look at one's girlfriend as a sex object'. Perhaps a bit too disquieting after all, the extraordinary suggestion is immediately succeeded by the reassuring remark that 'pretending to' will do just as well, providing that 'you are both young and beautiful, and do not underestimate the tantalizing effect your performance is intended to produce', that is to say, on men. For after dishing up some delightfully 'sick' rumours about Madonna and Sharon Stone, the story hastens to a predictable conclusion with a parting shot whose import could not be better articulated than in a comment from one of the interviewed 'designer dykes': 'OK, let's be honest about this. What could be the fun of making out with a woman if there were no men around eager to offer you a cure?' The glamorous 'lesbian lifestyle' turns out to be a rather mild affliction – nothing serious, nothing to worry about – for which a reliable remedy is easily available: the therapeutic sexual powers of (fortunately omnipresent) straight men.

The persistence with which the spectral lesbian is at once invoked and tends to disappear behind the mainstream cultural horizon first of all suggests that this specific borderline figure, the female psychosexual cross-over, must, notwithstanding appearances to the contrary, continue to be reduced to a negative semantic space in the collective imagination. But its unfailing reappearance in a variety of locations throughout Western history also attests to the considerable power this haunting figure persists in holding on the cultural consciousness. The fact that lesbianism, at present, has not merely been 'outed' within – as opposed to being left dangling at the margins of – the dominant cultural arena, but actually appears to be all over the place, furthermore signifies that the straight white male subject, whose formerly self-evident position is increasingly under attack from the various multiculturalisms indelibly colouring the contemporary social scene, can stave off his ensuing fears of disempowerment by simultaneously resurrecting *and* containing this particular figure of Otherness. Being deeply entrenched within the masculine psycho-system, it is, as I have pointed out before, precisely on account of its fantasmatic nature, as a product of male *Angst*, that the chimerical lesbian embodies the condition upon which the straight white male's emergence in the socio-symbolic order depends, whilst at the same time functioning as this order's vanishing-point. The unprecedented visibility of the 'new lesbian' in the dominant cultural domain is hence, it seems to me, both the product and a symptom of the current crisis spreading throughout the Western world, a collective identity crisis whose global implications first and foremost affect the upholders of white straight male supremacy. Within a pervasively multicultural social realm, it is the system of compulsory heterosexuality, which is, as we have noted, essentially a system of *female* heterosexuality, that must at all costs be maintained.

The dissimilarities in terms of genre, style and technique, which set films like *Bitter Moon* and *Basic Instinct* apart, thus do nothing to detract from the fact that the stories their respective directors choose to tell us are, in effect, strikingly similar. Indeed, whilst packaging their commodified products quite differently, in the final analysis these male fantasies do little more than offer us the Self/Same, age-old stories. In the following chapters, we shall see whether 'the lesbian' can indeed figure differently, that is, speak through and assume Other guises, in various forms of female fantasy. In doing so, we will turn our attention to fantasies that do not project themselves onto the big movie screen, but rather inscribe their unspeakable subject in and between the lines of a far less 'spectacular' medium, the respective discourses of the novel, and of critical theory.

4 Sex/textual Conflicts in *The Bell Jar*: Sylvia Plath's Doubling Negatives

> In psychotic depersonalization, the . . . subject's ego is no longer centred in its own body, and the body feels as if it has been taken over by others or is controlled by outside forces. When autoscopy occurs, the subject may see itself as it were from the outside or may be haunted by the most terrifying images, the *Doppelgänger*.
> Elizabeth Grosz, *Volatile Bodies*

Since its publication in 1963, the reputation of Sylvia Plath's *The Bell Jar* has acquired almost mythical proportions.[1] While Plath's life and premature death have been extensively documented over the years,[2] her semi-autobiographical novel has become one of the classic twentieth-century stories of female adolescence, enjoying virtual cult status with both readers and literary critics.[3] Taken up by the early women's movement, *The Bell Jar*'s protagonist, Plath's *alter ego* Esther Greenwood, has frequently served as the embodiment of female victimization in the pre-liberation days of the 1950s and early 1960s.[4] Feminist critics have seen in this tale of madness and self-destruction a harrowing account of growing up female in post-war middle-class America,[5] finding it one of the most powerful indictments of the so-called double standard that made many young female lives miserable at the time; in other words, a splendid exposition of what is so aptly captured in Betty Friedan's phrase the 'feminine mystique'.[6]

In mainstream literary history, *The Bell Jar* generally figures as the 'female counter-part' to that other quintessentially American story of post-war 'alienation and disengagement', J. D. Salinger's

The Catcher in the Rye (1951).[7] In fact, as Linda Wagner-Martin has pointed out, Plath used this classic male quest narrative as a model for what was to become her own, turning to Salinger's novel for structure, and drawing on it 'whenever she ran out of events that seemed to fit Esther's story.'[8] Although such comments should warn us against reading *The Bell Jar* as a direct reflection of the author's life, Plath's various biographers and her posthumously published letters and journals confirm that the novel is largely autobiographical in content.[9] Compounded by the author's suicide a few months after the book came out, its autobiographical groundings have undeniably enhanced *The Bell Jar*'s sensational impact, an impact which does not appear to have diminished during its more than thirty-year history.

What could be the incentive, or perhaps even the point, of attempting to reread a text which is so well known and so exhaustively analysed that it seems to have become almost common property? Moreover, and considering the novel's longstanding feminist appropriation, what could be the purpose of doing so from a lesbian perspective? What I propose to do in this chapter is to perform a 'perverse reading' of *The Bell Jar*, to approach it as a narrative of female adolescence in which it is not in the first place the operations of *gender*-ideology, but rather the conflicts of female (hetero)sexuality that play a structural part. In other words, to draw out the story's ambivalent sexual subtext, which forms not only its own 'unsaid', but also that of most feminist readings of it.

The figure of the lesbian makes a phantom-like yet critical appearance in *The Bell Jar* on various textual levels, asserting its disruptive potential in two striking ways: first, by complicating and unsettling the relationship between the narrator and her protagonist, and second, by surfacing in the guise of the 'most terrifying of images', the *Doppelgänger*. Whereas the focus of my discussion will be on specific complexities offered by and in the text, I will additionally consider those contextual factors that are crucial to such a 'perverse', that is to say, lesbian understanding of its signifying operations.

A first illuminating extra-textual detail is couched in the history of the novel's publication. While she was working on it, Plath wrote to a friend that she 'enjoyed writing the book,' that she had, indeed, 'never been so excited about anything else she had written.' Its impressive reputation may easily lead us to forget, however, that Plath later called *The Bell Jar* a 'pot-boiler' and first had it published under the pseudonym of Victoria Lucas.[10] To resolve such apparent contradictions in the author's feelings about her all-time bestseller, Anne Stevenson notes that Plath at the time insisted that she did not wish to link her name as a poet to such a prosaic piece of work. Obviously not quite satisfied with this explanation, Stevenson then goes on to attribute Plath's reluctance to publish under her own name to a need for 'discretion', a desire she considers quite understandable in view of the 'barely disguised, hurtful portrait of her mother' the novel presents, on top of the 'portrayal ... of a devastating period in [the author's] own personal history'. But even these presumed grounds for the option of anonymity appear inadequate, for in a footnote Stevenson informs us that 'toward the end of her life [Plath] abandoned this discretion and spoke of the novel to several London friends.' She unfortunately refrains from giving us any clues as to the cause of this shift in the author's attitude.[11]

In remarkable contrast to these 'exonerating' observations, Wagner-Martin asserts that writing *The Bell Jar* was a 'liberating experience' for Plath, whilst further suggesting that the author's *alter ego* Esther is 'not ashamed of her descent into madness; she wants to tell about it, partly to rid herself of memories, partly to help other women faced with the same cultural pressure' which precipitated her mental breakdown.[12] In trying to account for the author's desire for anonymity, Wagner-Martin points to the ambivalent portrayal of not just the mother figure, but of all the older female characters in the novel, whom she identifies exclusively in their function as unreliable teachers or dubious role models. Despite the fact that the intertextual paradigm of the 'young girl/older woman', or the 'pupil-teacher relationship', forms one of the central topoi in the fragmented tradition of lesbian literature,[13] Wagner-Martin apparently feels no need to probe into the underlying causes or the specific quality of the ambivalence characterizing Esther's relations with these older females.[14] Nor does she seem to perceive that a similar kind of ambiguity suffuses the protagonist's strained relationships with female characters her own age. Yet it is precisely in the equivocal depiction of these variously strained same-sex relationships that a more persuasive answer to the question of the author's willingness to lay claim to her 'pot-boiler' would seem to lie. I will come back to this shortly.

Another significant detail in the history of its publication, one that is equally likely to be obscured by *The Bell Jar*'s present-day prominence in the American canon, is the fact that the manuscript was accepted by its original British publisher only after several editors in the US had rejected it. Whilst Plath's decision to use a pseudonym can be read as a deliberate act to disengage herself from this 'transposed autobiography', the text was thus subjected to a further, in this case externally-imposed, divorce from its author, making its official début not in her native country but in that in which she was at the time cast in the role of resident alien.[15] The atmosphere of disconnection and estrangement marking the novel's history from the beginning, acquires, as I hope to show, distinct significance in retrospect. For the moment, it is furthermore interesting to note that the two female American editors who refused the manuscript did so – 'kindly but with apt criticism', Stevenson approvingly remarks – on account of the fact that Esther Greenwood's 'experience remain[ed] a private one'.[16] Clearly, any awareness of the 'feminine mystique' – or of what would later be captured in the feminist slogan 'the personal is the political' – had not yet entered New York editorial offices.

When the book was eventually launched by Heinemann on 14 January, 1963, none of the reviews that subsequently appeared in the British press was 'entirely adverse'. Most critics' responses show remarkable agreement in at least one respect, however: all felt that the author had not succeeded in 'establishing a viewpoint'.[17] While generally considered a serious flaw, it is this very same 'problem' of perspective which, we shall see, is not only closely entwined with the ambivalence characterizing the female interrelationships central to the protagonist's quest, but which additionally allows us to perceive the connections between the narrative perspective and the sexual conflicts and contradictions operating on the novel's variously interacting textual levels. To further explore these connections, I will first briefly discuss the relationship between the narrator and her protagonist – or to use Gérard Genette's somewhat opaque but more precise terms, between the extradiegetic and the intradiegetic levels of the text – in order subsequently to concentrate on the figure of the *Doppelgänger* or 'double'.[18]

In rereading *The Bell Jar* – or, for that matter, any other text by a not self-identified lesbian author – in the context of a study on configurations of lesbian sexuality,[19] I am not necessarily, or even primarily, concerned with the representation or portrayal of lesbian characters; nor, I should add, is it my objective (posthumously) to establish the 'truth' about such authors' sexual orientations. By focusing, in contrast, on textual figures and figurations that in some way suggest, in Marilyn Frye's words, a specific 'mode of disloyalty' towards the heteropatriarchal order, I am employing a notion of lesbian sexuality that first of all designates a disruptive material phenomenon with regard to the smooth operations of 'Phallocratic Reality'. On a more abstract, symbolic level the figure of the lesbian additionally represents, as Judith Roof has convincingly argued, the 'vanishing point' of Eurowestern metaphysics as such. Such 'disloyalty' to prevailing systems of thought in cultural production itself may hence also serve as an enabling analytical tool in critical practice. Let me briefly digress to illuminate the grounds for these assumptions.

Drawing on a diversity of discourses – from cinema and psychoanalysis to literature and literary criticism – the project of Roof's appropriately entitled book, *A Lure of Knowledge*, comprises a sustained and thought-provoking effort at disentangling the paradoxical (non)existence of lesbian sexuality in Western culture. Through a meticulous exploration of a large number of both male- and female-authored texts, she succeeds in bringing to light a range of 'similar rhetorical or argumentative positions' *vis-à-vis* lesbian sexuality, whose specific contextualization leads her to the following conclusion:

> Operating as points of systemic failure, configurations of lesbian sexuality often reflect the complex incongruities that occur when the logic or philosophy of a system becomes self-contradictory, visibly fails to account for something, or cannot complete itself.[20]

Highlighting the overdetermined nature of such configurations, Roof makes clear that lesbian sexuality does not only upset the logic of dominant conceptual frameworks, but that the subject 'simultaneously . . . instigates the overtly compensatory and highly visible return of the terms of the ruptured system that mend and mask its gaps'. Since the threat of exposure embodied by the 'female invert' can be directly traced to the figure's undefinability, she further infers that 'attempts to depict or explain lesbian sexuality spur anxieties about knowledge and identity.' As a result, the configurations of lesbianism in the variety of (straight) discourses under investigation can be seen to function as 'complex representations whose particular location in a text . . . reveal not lesbian sexuality *per se*, but the anxieties it produces.'[21]

Precisely because of its significance as a fundamental disloyalty to a hierarchical system of (hetero)sexual gender relations, lesbian sexuality poses a threat of confusion to the 'straight mind' that frames Western social reality. It simultaneously constitutes the moment at which the fundamental contradictions of, to recall Irigaray's provocative term, the hom(m)osexual symbolic order most conspicuously reveal themselves.[22] This not only holds true for such obviously male fantasies as, for instance, the films discussed in the preceding two chapters. The lesbian's destabilizing, 'complificating' effects also become apparent when we consider the various discursive figures under whose guise her 'unnatural' desires tend to surface in female-authored texts, especially in those pre-dating the liberatory era of the late 1960s.[23]

As covert articulations of the 'love that dare not speak its name', it is primarily, we recall, through complexly veiled and often recurring patterns of imagery that lesbian desire speaks through the overtly heterosexual surface in pre-, or proto-feminist female fictions. What is 'unnameable' emerges in the contradictory 'nodal points' structuring a given narrative, discursive knots which acquire the significance of, to quote Roof again, 'conflicting impetuses of representational insufficiency and recuperation'. To her list of such configurations – which includes 'titillating foreplay, simulated heterosexuality, exotic excess, knowing center, joking inauthenticity, artful compromise, and masculine masks' – I wish to add the figure of the female adolescent.[24] Functioning in the Western cultural imagination as an emblem of indefiniteness and ambiguity, the figure of the female adolescent, as I will try to show here and in the following chapter, may operate in (pre-liberation) women's literature as both a mask for and a signal of an unstable and transgressive, that is, lesbian sex/textuality.

The concept of adolescence as a stage of development with explicitly sexual connotations is of relatively recent date.[25] While the Romantic Age can be considered to have given birth to the category of the child – think of Rousseau's *Émile* (1762) – it was the work of the sexologists at the end of the ninteenth century, and the dissemination of (Freudian) psychoanalytic theory at the beginning of the twentieth, that produced the notion of adolescence as we know it.[26] In Foucaultian terms, it was thus with the 'invention of sexuality' as such, that the adolescent entered our discursive universe as a recognizable type, a specific kind of human being. Conceived of as an essentially transitional phenomenon, adolescence was subsequently recognized as a crucial stage in identity formation precisely on account of its sexual overdetermination, as an intermediate period during which the relatively unsexed child develops into a sexually fully-differentiated adult subject. Encompassing an inevitable but passing psychosexual crisis, the task of adolescence is successfully completed with the individual's 'espousal' and internalization of either of two culturally acceptable forms of adult subjecthood, that is to say, when s/he adopts on a subjective, psychic level what are in effect culturally constructed images of 'masculinity' and 'femininity' respectively.[27]

Whereas the locus of twentieth-century definitions of identity thus in the first instance appears to reside in a person's sexuality, the institutionalization of nineteenth-century medico-scientific discourses has, paradoxically, succeeded in shifting attention away from sexuality to gender. In line with prevalent biological and psychological notions regarding puberty, adolescence is today generally regarded as a period of mental as well as emotional confusion, of (sexual) experimentation, and overall irresponsibility. As a 'privileged' timespace in Western consumer culture, adolescence or 'youth' represents a stage of licensed rebellion ultimately aimed at setting the individual on her/his way to her/his future role in the social order. By positing a direct and causal relationship between the biological body, psychosexuality and gender, the discourse of adolescence has thus itself become another of what Foucault calls 'technologies of the self', ushering children of either sex into their adult positions as gendered subjects.[28]

In traditional literary terms, it is the genre of the *Bildungsroman* or novel of development which centres on this critical phase of subjective formation. Depicting the hero/ine's quest for her/his self, such narrative itineraries are usually characterized by a strong sense of dislocation.[29] Organized around a protagonist overwhelmed by feelings of meaninglessness and incoherence, adolescent novels present often disconcerting accounts of disorder on which an omniscient narrator, firmly established in her/his position as an adult speaking subject, retrospectively imposes order. From its opening sentence onwards, *The Bell Jar* conforms to this pattern: 'It was a queer, sultry summer, the summer they electrocuted the Rosenbergs, and I didn't know what I was doing in New York' (1). Situating the narrative in a specific moment in the past, the sense of disconnection expressed in the latter part of this sentence immediately acquires a gruesome dimension by the preceding reference to the Rosenbergs. Invoking an atmosphere of betrayal, death and destruction, the narrator forges an unequivocal link between her former Self and the socio-political context: 'It had nothing to do with me, but I couldn't help wondering what it would be like, being burned alive all along your nerves' (1). Having observed that 'something was wrong' with her at the time, she proceeds by emphatically establishing a distance between this nineteen-year-old girl – feeling 'still and very empty, the way the eye of a tornado must feel' (3) – and herself, shifting to a later moment at which she 'was all right again', and on to the narrative present. We learn that this later Self still keeps material objects from the past 'around the house' and only 'last week' brought them out again 'for the baby to play with' (4). By demarcating her present Self in precisely these terms, the narrator not only makes clear that nothing is 'wrong' with her anymore, she also discretely conveys that she is currently fulfilling her proper role as a wife and mother. By implicitly yet effectively linking the return of sanity to motherhood, the text thus foregrounds the suggestion that the 'recovery' of the narrator's *alter ego* is located first and foremost in the acquisition of a 'normal' gender identity.

While a deliberate distancing between the narrator and her/his protagonist is a feature characteristic of most novels of development, the clash between the disturbing narrative events of *The Bell Jar*, between Esther Greenwood's story of madness and despair, and the jauntily sarcastic, even cynical tone of voice in which it is rendered, is quite extreme. The novel's high degree of artistic control and its self-deprecating sense of irony appear to point up a need to set up a complex defence system against the disconcerting contents of the story. The narrator's show of discursive authority hence simultaneously serves to ascertain symbolic agency, and to contain the threat of disintegration posed by the inscription of insanity in the text itself and in the narrative's constituting events.

The tension resulting from the interplay between these two textual levels has, I think correctly, been analysed by feminist critics as a reflection of the contradictory demands made upon women by and within patriarchal ideology.[30] Still, even though I have no wish to imply that gender is *not* relevant to Esther Greenwood's predicament, I do think that too little critical attention has been paid to her story's sexual undercurrents. By privileging the category of gender, feminist readings of *The Bell Jar* have not so much neglected as actually obscured the powerful sexual subtext underpinning the narrative. As suggested before, it is this fraught sexual subtext, even more than gender conflicts, which structurally informs the novel's discordant discourse.

Since sexuality largely obtains on the level of the unconscious, a psychoanalytic approach to the novel of adolescence would appear most viable to assess the relation between its author-narrator and her subject matter. In psychic terms, adolescence is induced by the re-emerging Oedipal depression at the end of the latency period. It entails a reawakening of the repressed desire for the primary love object, which, in Western societies organized around the nuclear family, is the mother for subjects of either sex. Prompted by the onset of puberty, the adolescent quest is aimed at the recovery of a second love object.

The French psychoanalyst and critical theorist Julia Kristeva contends that the psychosexual crisis known as adolescence involves a resurgence of repressed pre-symbolic or imaginary

material 'in the aftermath of the oedipal stabilization of subjective identity'.[31] This destabilization of her/his subjective identity,
she posits, leads the adolescent to a renewed questioning of
her/his identifications 'along with his [sic] capacities for speech
and symbolization'. As an 'open structure' personality, the adolescent hence 'maintains a renewable identity', having access to
imaginary material which in Western culture is granted to the
adult 'only as a reader or spectator . . . or as artist'. Directing her
focus to narrative fiction, Kristeva goes on to submit that the
activity of writing adolescence consequently 'permit[s] a genuine
inscription of unconscious contents within language', while the
act of fictionalizing simultaneously serves as a 'powerful screen
against madness'. The genre of novel, as an open structure *par
excellence*, is largely 'tributary to the "adolescent" economy', and
can thus serve to accommodate the re-emergence of repressed
unconscious contents as well enable its symbolic recollection in a
process of psychic reorganization. The adolescent novel, Kristeva
concludes, allows the writing subject to 're-elaborate his psychic
space' while the authorial narrator, with her/his unrestrained
power over characters, action and plot, at the same time functions
as a forceful ordering principle to protect her/him 'from phobic
affects'.[32]

Singling out the adolescent as a '*topos* of incompleteness that is
also that of all possibilities', the altogether celebratory vein in
which Kristeva describes the polyvalence of adolescent writing no
doubt partly derives from her unwavering bias for male-authored
texts.[33] By not considering any female-authored adolescent novels, she is able conveniently to gloss over the fundamental contradictions marking female sexuality from its earliest stages
onwards. Such contradictions, while ingrained in the normative
process of female heterosexuality as a whole, would appear to
make themselves felt with a vengeance during the adolescent
crisis.

Within the context of normative heterosexuality, the Oedipal
crisis for the little girl involves not only the abandonment of her
desire for the first love object and its redirection to an object of
the opposite sex, but also the enforced identification with the
position of inferiority of the (now devalued) mother. Taken
together, the loss of the original object and the girl's recognition

of her constitution in lack, acquire, to borrow a phrase of Kaja Silverman's, the significance of 'major surgery'.[34] Surely a re-emergence of this highly traumatic experience cannot but painfully inculcate upon the female subject the founding split in her Self, the split caused by the irreconcilability of her need for symbolic agency on the one hand, and her desire for the primary object on the other. Since a female same-sex object choice falls virtually outside the realm of the patriarchal symbolic, it seems likely that these oppositional desires will significantly qualify the writing of *female* adolescence, as compared to what in Kristeva's book evidently goes for adolescent writing *per se*, that is, male adolescent writing. And, I propose, it is the split between the desire for discursive control and the forbidden desire for the female love object which, by extension, accounts for the palpable friction between the intra- and the extradiegetic levels that tends to characterize female quest narratives.

The strained intensity marking the discourse of *The Bell Jar* can be seen to signal precisely the kind of 'systemic failure' that, as Roof suggests, allows us to locate 'configurations of lesbian sexuality' in ostensibly straight narrative surfaces. The metaphor of 'speaking in tongues', a phrase not infrequently used in relation to lesbian writing, conveys that the irreconcilability of 'abnormal' desires with the rules and conventions of sex/textual normality discloses itself primarily on the level of discourse. Realized in a splitting-off of markedly discrepant voices, the psychic causes and, by implication, the effects of such discursive fragmentation are nonetheless rather more serious than what readers today have learned to recognize as the self-conscious multivoicedness or 'carnivaleque heteroglossia' characteristic of postmodern texts.[35]

At an early point in the novel, *The Bell Jar*'s narrator, finding herself being addressed by two different names in two different voices, seemingly jokingly remarks that it is 'as if [she] had a split personality or something' (22). In view of the specific nature and primary aims of the adolescent process, that is, the acquisition of a recognizable socio-cultural identity as a gendered individual, the profound sense of confusion and extreme self-consciousness that lies behind this remark is not really surprising. Indeed, as Susan J. Douglas observes, 'there's little doubt that a pathological level of self-consciousness is what being an adolescent is all about, at least in America.'[36] Douglas, partly reminiscing about her own adolescence, partly engaging in social historiography, traces the origins of this national trait to an important shift in US history, to the rise of consumer culture in the post-war period. The source of such pathology, she argues, should be sought primarily in the influence of the mass media, and especially of the popular magazines directing themselves specifically to young girls, which began flooding the American market in the 1950s and 1960s. Highly popular publications like *Seventeen*, *Glamour* and *Mademoiselle* hugely 'exaggerated [girls'] psychic schizophrenia', being 'schizophrenic' themselves 'about whether to approach [them] as if [they] were coherent, unified individuals or a bundle of contradictory, inchoate multiple personalities'.[37] Autobiographical sources reveal that Plath drew on her own stint as a guest editor of *Mademoiselle* to describe her *alter ego*'s summer in New York City: in the novel's opening section, Esther is staying as one of a group of female guest editors of a fashion magazine called *Ladies' Day*. Uttered by a temporary resident in the homeland of such cultural confusion, the flippant remark concerning Esther's personality would appear poignantly to underscore Douglas's observations. The multiplication of differences in our own multicultural times should therefore not prevent us from sufficiently recognizing the profound anxiety lying behind it.

The reference to the protagonist's 'split personality' takes on even more disturbing significance when we further take into account the novel's wider socio-historical context. As one among a number of psychoanalytic concepts that today belong to most people's everyday vocabulary, such pseudo-scientific terms, but also more strictly clinical ones, like schizophrenia and hysteria, were introduced to the general public only some fifty years ago; that is to say, when the rapidly expanding purview of the mass media, in particular television, facilitated the popular dissemination of all sorts of 'specialist' discourses. Whilst Freud's ideas had for a long time been available to various contingents of 'experts' (including medical doctors, intellectuals, writers and philosophers), it was only in the post-war era that psychoanalysis became a virtual lay discourse, setting firm foot in the public domain of industrialized societies at large, and on both sides of the Atlantic.

Moreover, the post-war vulgarization of Freud's work did not only result in the kinds of 'normalizing cures' that have given American psychoanalytic practice such a bad name. It also grew in the reactionary 1950s, into one of the most effective and widely used repressive tools of socio-political control.

Whilst the postmodern celebration of difference may easily allow us to overlook the anxiety-ridden psychic subtext of Esther's story, the collapse of the Berlin Wall, and its symbolic value with regard to East-West relations, might equally cause us to neglect the significance of the repressive political climate in which the story is set, that is, the Cold War and its incisive effects on people's personal lives. Exposed to the so-called Communist threat that defined the overall parameters of the Cold War era, in the course of the 1950s, Americans in all walks of life were subjected to what was, in the final instance, a system of virtual national surveillance. The immense impact of the public tribunals to which formerly well-respected individuals were summoned (accused of engaging in such un-American activities as adhering to progressive political ideas), to a considerable extent resulted from the fact that the secret surveillance of citizenry was being engineered and channelled through the mass media. The 'Red scare' literally entered into ordinary people's homes.

Foregrounding the structural significance of *The Bell Jar*'s socio-historical context, Pat MacPherson pertinently observes that by the mid-1950s the norm, that is, 'a single-dimensional conformity based on image', seemed to have 'achieved the status of official language' in US society. At the height of Senator McCarthy's power, 'those speaking a different language were by definition Alien.'[38] Rhetorically dividing the world into Us and Them, McCarthy's system of public persecution was geared to securing social conformity by disseminating a nationwide scare around what J. Edgar Hoover, director of the FBI, termed 'the enemy within'.[39] The power politics effected by a 'mass communication system unprecedented in history' at the same time proved to be the most pervasive ideological state apparatus to date.[40] Propelled into positions in which mental health equalled social adjustment, MacPherson suggests, 'each citizen was set self-policing to enact a "fulfilled" conformity convincing to others if always fraudulent to oneself.' The paranoia proceeding from this enforced yet 'basic psychic dishonesty' urged individual subjects to seek 'only external screens on which to project the denied self and call it the Other'.[41] Given the atmosphere of demonization and criminalization that has traditionally surrounded practices and activities associated with 'perverse desire', it should come as no surprise that McCarthy's America, as Katie King has pointed out, saw a thorough intertwining of the 'spectres of homosexuality and communism'.[42] With even the suspicion of disloyalty to the Law rendered a potentially criminal act, openly deviating from the sexual norm would indisputably have appeared, to the majority of the American public, no less than suicidal.

It is the all-encompassing sway of the phrase 'the enemy within' which establishes the link between Esther Greenwood and the Rosenbergs. The paranoid concept additionally marks, though slightly less straightforwardly, the connection between the adolescent protagonist's sense of her 'split personality' and the figure of the lesbian, in its historical function as a repressed psychosexual Other in Western culture. In view of Plath's frequently noted preoccupation with 'doubles', finally, the notion of 'the enemy within' acquires particular significance when set against a background in which ideological scapegoating was a policy practised on a national scale.

In psychoanalytic terms, the setting up of (imaginary) *Doppelgängers* or doubles serves to screen the subject against unwanted or anxiety-ridden aspects of or in her/himself, allowing her/him to displace such negative aspects onto (an) external Other(s). Similarly, or so argues Robert Rogers in an early study of the phenomenon, in literary texts the figure of the double generally represents a character 'which may be thought of ... as directly portraying, or indirectly generated by, conflict which is intrapsychic or endopsychic' to the author, or to her/his unmarked textual representative, the author-narrator.[43] Such literary doubling may take multiple forms, different aspects of the author's Self may be transformed into a number of different characters that represent a variety of 'conflicting drives, orientations, or attitudes'.[44] Splittings of the Self are not restricted to the inner psyche; or rather, the inner psyche does not function as a sort of self-contained unity that merely acts in response to the outside world. Psychic formations are structurally informed, if not constituted, by the operations of the (external) culture in which they obtain. Hence the frequent 'inclination of the racist' to '[adopt] social myths as a mode of dealing with his own inner tension and insecurity'.[45]

To elucidate the complex underpinnings of fictional doubling, Rogers attempts to draw an analogy between the 'phenomenon of decomposition in literature' and the neurotic's strategy of psychic dissociation or depersonalization. Writing in the late 1960s, he apparently had little evidence to go on, and obviously was (or felt) able to maintain that 'decomposition remains a minor concept in psychoanalytic theory.' Cases of 'autoscopic vision and multiple personality' – the principal counterparts of decomposition in clinical practice – had, he contends, as yet 'not been encountered' by practising psychoanalysts.[46] The spate of medico-scientific publications on Multiple Personality Disorder (MPD) that have been flooding the market in recent years would appear to signify a dramatic change in this respect.[47] Indeed, it may not be entirely coincidental that it is only now, when the diffracting effects of the 'cultural crisis' jointly occasioned by postmodernism and the ending of the Cold War are making themselves felt in the popular domain, that the so-called decentred subject of deconstructive theory has also been fully acknowledged in its clinical guise.

The relative prevalence of MPD in (female) patients who have, at some point in their lives, suffered from sexual abuse or incest, indicates that the syndrome, as a complex psychic defence system consisting in a splitting up of the Self into several, more or less independent, partial selves or *'alters'*, entails extreme measures of self-repression and potential self-mutilation. Seen in this light, Rogers' description of the double as the outcome of an 'inner, emotional split, an ambivalence generated out of his own confusion about his identity' seems decidedly underplayed.[48] Such an appreciation of the *Doppelgänger* comes, in effect, very close to what psychiatrist Erik Erikson has popularized as the 'normal' crisis structure of adolescence.[49] The often sexual underpinnings of psychic dissociation, or clinical MPD, would nonetheless appear to corroborate Rogers' claim that there is an indissoluble connection between paranoia and the 'narcissistic phenomenon' of doubling, a point of intersection which manifests itself in the 'mechanism of projection ... common to both'. The existence of such links between sexuality, doubling and paranoia forms the underlying ground of my supposition that it is in the multiple figurations of *The Bell Jar*'s adolescent protagonist that the inscription of insanity in its narrative surface converges with its conflictual sexual subtext.

At some point during her enervating stay in New York City with *Ladies' Day*, Esther Greenwood consciously assumes the fictive identity of 'Elly Higginbottom ... from Chicago', in order to feel 'safer' in the unwonted cosmopolitan world of the big city. Whilst such a deliberate act of protective dissociation is a fairly common phenomenon in people living under stress, three major doubles figure in the text that represent the kind of genuine psychic split-offs or *alters* of the (unconscious) Self manifested in multiple personalities.

The first of these *alters* is Doreen, a luscious Southern belle whom the narrator retrospectively 'guess[es]' to have been 'one of [her] troubles' (4). Described in unmistakably erotic terms, Doreen at once functions as the object of the narrator's younger Self's aggressive sexual desires – '[She] had an interesting, slightly sweaty smell that reminded me of those scallopy leaves of sweet fern you break off and crush between your fingers for the musk of them' (6) – and figures as an object of identificatory investment: 'Everything [Doreen] said was like a secret voice speaking straight out of my bones' (7). The contradiction implied in these observations is rendered explicit when Doreen, with her 'bright, white hair standing out in a cotton candy fluff round her head and blue eyes like transparent agate marbles' (4–5), is envisaged as the positive image of femininity in relation to which the narrator differentiates her own former Self as its negative counterpart: 'With her white hair and white dress [Doreen] was so white she looked silver ... I felt myself melting into the shadows like a negative of a person I'd never seen before in my life' (10). While her double's unrestrained sensuality and sexual escapades alternately make Esther feel like a 'small black dot' and a 'hole in the ground' (17), what she has learned to regard as the Other's wanton promiscuity at the same time fills her with a profound sense of guilt and disgust. In order to dissociate herself from the attractions of 'Doreen's body', which she perceives as the 'concrete testimony of [her] own dirty nature', Esther frequently purges herself by taking hot baths: 'I guess I feel about a hot bath the way ... religious people feel about holy water' (21). Producing a complex mixture of feelings, ranging from an acute sense of inadequacy to physical attraction and repulsion, Doreen embodies the stereotypical image of Woman as flesh, simultaneous source of temptation and object of damnation, and thus represents one of the stock figures of normative femininity, at once imposed and forbidden by the Paternal Law.[50]

Set off as a foil to 'bad girl' Doreen, we encounter another of Esther's doubles in 'good girl' Betsy, who seems 'imported straight from Kansas with her bouncing blonde pony-tail and Sweetheart-of-Sigma-Chi-smile' (6). The incarnation of innocence, of all-American girlishness, of clean and healthy virginity (the narrator wryly observes that 'pureness was the great issue' when she was nineteen), Esther treasures this Other as her most inner Self: 'Deep down, I would be loyal to Betsy ... It was Betsy I resembled at heart' (24). As flip sides of the coin stamped patriarchal womanhood, the two oppositional sets of sexual values personified by these doubles symbolize the incompatible demands imposed on female subjects by the heterosexual gender system, the resulting contradictions of which are so adequately reflected in the protagonist's name.[51]

Introduced at an early point in the text, Esther's third double Joan Gilling gradually gains significance. She begins to figure prominently only when the protagonist's increasing mental disorder, culminating in a nearly successful suicide attempt, has issued in her commitment to a psychiatric hospital. Joan – 'big as a horse' and a former 'college hockey champion' – is unsympathetically portrayed throughout. With her 'teeth like tombstones', her 'breathy voice', and her keenness on 'doing things out-of-doors' (61), she is immediately recognizable as a horrifying example of the stereotypical 'mannish lesbian'.[52] While the narrator takes great pains to distance her former Self from the alien Other, Esther's suggested 'schizophrenia' is thus from the first tightly linked up with a figure consistently presented in terms which invoke the pathological notion of female inversion. As if to underline the contrast between the protagonist's 'masculine' and her 'feminine' doubles respectively, the text initially suggests that it is Joan, with her 'pale, pebble eyes', who identifies with Esther rather than the other way around.

The 'female invert' miraculously shows up in the mental hospital where Esther has been taken after her forcible resurrection to life. She claims to have cut her wrists upon reading about Esther in the newspaper, an act which gives the latter the idea that they 'might have something in common' (212). Esther's subjection to the psychiatric 'discipline of normalization' (treatment consists of large doses of insulin supplemented with electro-shock therapy) has by then effectively broken her spirit. Identified as the 'beaming double of [her] old best self', Joan presently breaks the spell of passivity in which the protagonist has been caught up since her hospitalization. Awakening her from the stupor brought about by what was, at the time, a not unusual medical regime, the repulsive sexual Other enables Esther's intellectual and artistic aspirations to re-emerge. But with the resurrection of these 'masculine' ambitions, the old fear of 'feminine' inadequacy also returns, leading Esther to suspect that this 'old best self' is something 'specially designed to follow and torment' her (217).

Alternately taking up a position as object and as subject in the ensuing desirous and identificatory interchange between herself and her double, Esther's feelings toward Joan remain utterly ambivalent, as does the narrator's tone in describing their curious bond. Although the 'unspeakable' word is never actually mentioned, the precise nature of this ambivalence is indirectly disclosed by numerous references to lesbian sexuality generally, and in connection with Joan in particular, which surface with growing frequency in the latter half of the text.

The narrator's penchant for blunt statement and direct description conspicuously falters on the negative semantic space of female same-sex desire. When Joan tells Esther about her close relations with one of the older women haunting the latter's imagination, that is, the mother of her former boyfriend Buddy Willard, the gap in the narrator's discourse is typographically rendered in a series of full stops: 'Joan and Mrs Willard. Joan . . . and Mrs Willard . . .'. The suggestive value of these dots is revealed in a roundabout way when, without further transition, the narrator continues to relate an event occurring earlier that day, allowing the ground of her former Self's obsessions to be disclosed by association. Getting no answer to her knock on another patient's door, Esther had 'stepped into [DeeDee's] room', fully aware of the fact that she was transgressing against the most fundamental of unspoken hospital rules:

> At Belsize, even at Belsize, the doors had locks, but the patients had no keys. A shut door meant privacy, and was respected, like a locked door. One knocked and knocked again, then went away. I remembered this as I stood, my eyes half-useless after the brilliance of the hall, in the room's deep, musky dark. (230)

Urged on by her wish to know, to solve the riddle of what 'women and women – would be actually doing', hoping for 'some revelation of specific evil', Esther's transgression brings her face to face with what she desires to see but cannot consciously register; an 'unspeakable' secret, moreover, which the narrator, even in retrospect, cannot depict in anything but veiled terms:

> As my vision cleared, I saw a shape rise from the bed ... The shape adjusted its hair, and two pale, pebble eyes regarded me through the gloom. DeeDee lay back on the pillows, bare-legged under her green wool dressing-gown, and watched me with a little mocking smile. (230–1)

After this unnerving yet mesmerizing incident, Joan's function as the protagonist's most haunting Other becomes ever more pronounced. The latter's need to alienate her Self from her inverted *Doppelgänger* continues to grow in equal measure, until even looking at Joan gives Esther a 'creepy feeling', as if she were 'observing a Martian, or a particularly warty toad'. The closer she comes to an acknowledgement of her fascination with the sexual Other, the stronger her need to distance herself from Joan's 'thoughts and feelings', which are literally presented as 'a wry black image of [her] own' (231). While evoking the connotations of negativity and inversion surrounding the lesbian in the Western cultural imagination generally, the striking resemblance between this image of blackness and the view of her former Self as the 'negative' of the white, bright embodiment of female heterosexuality, Doreen, becomes all the more suggestive when the narrator subsequently admits: 'Sometimes I wondered if I had made Joan up. Other times I wondered if she would pop in at every crisis of my life' (231). Since it is evidently her double's inverted sexuality that poses the most fundamental threat to Esther's frenzied attempts at 'practic[ing her] new, normal personality' (238), it is not really surprising that, with the protagonist's increasingly successful 'normalization', Joan's mental health deteriorates. In the end, the negative Other is quite literally killed off: in the penultimate chapter we learn that she has 'hanged herself' (248).[53]

This act of narrative erasure with respect to the 'wry black image' of sexual inversion forms the culmination of a string of similar displacements, a sequence of narrative and discursive dissociations which may have found its starting-point in *The Bell Jar*'s extra-textual, or pre-textual, history. But as her survival as a character suggests, the lesbian Other's disappearance from Esther's story may not be as definitive an obliteration as it would seem. Indeed, the spectre of the invert continues to haunt the text, for the ambivalence surrounding the *Doppelgänger* identified as the protagonist's 'old best self', is, despite her elimination on the novel's intradietetic level, sustained on its extradiegetic level. The narrator's unabating struggle with 'the enemy within' is unmistakably conveyed by the sequence depicting the scene of Joan's funeral:

> At the altar the coffin loomed in its snow-pallor of flowers – the black shadow of something that wasn't there ... That shadow would marry this shadow, and the peculiar, yellowish soil of our locality seal the wound in the whiteness, and yet another snowfall erase the traces of newness in Joan's grave ... All during the simple funeral service I wondered what I was burying. (256)

In the light of the foregoing 'perverse' reading of the text, the black and white imagery controlling this passage would in itself seem adequately to support my contention that it is a conflictual sexuality which lies 'buried' beneath *The Bell Jar*'s 'normalized' surface structure. It is, however, the narrator's retrospective self-questioning which conclusively accounts for the profound anxiety, articulated in the text's disparate discursive operations, which was apparently recognized, though perhaps not consciously, by the

American publishers who rejected Plath's manuscript on account of its failure to 'establish a viewpoint'. Placed within its socio-political context, I think we can safely assume that the *The Bell Jar* was not only considered unfit for publication because it called into question the myth of all-American womanhood. Plath's 'pot-boiler', the writing of which was supposedly such a liberating experience, was also, perhaps primarily, unacceptable because its subversive sexual subtext threatened to expose the 'wound in the whiteness' of normative female heterosexuality as such. And that specific form of sex/textual unaccountability was, in the USA of the early 1960s, obviously altogether intolerable. The next chapter will show that, at a different time and a different place, some female authors did succeed in positively inscribing lesbian desire into ostensibly straight(forward) narrative texts – and got away with it.

5 Queer Undercurrents: Disruptive Desire in Elizabeth Bowen's *Friends and Relations*

> The writer, like a swimmer caught by an undertow, is borne in an unexpected direction. He is carried to a subject which has awaited him – a subject sometimes no part of his conscious plan. Reality, the reality of sensation, has accumulated where it was least sought. To write is to be captured – captured by some experience to which one may have hardly given a thought.
>
> Elizabeth Bowen, Preface to *The Last September*

Thinking about pre-liberation 'lesbian' authors, the name of the Anglo-Irish novelist and short-story-writer Elizabeth Bowen (1899–1972) is not the first to come to mind. If remembered at all, or actually acknowledged as a not insignificant figure on the early twentieth-century English literary scene, Bowen is usually placed among a gallery of 'minor writers', male as well as female, whose work has been largely overshadowed by the (overwhelmingly male) luminaries of High Modernism. Nor is Bowen's name likely to be associated with the group of female authors who, in the course of several decades of feminist critical practice, have been claimed as her 'Sapphic' contemporaries,[1] such as token female modernist Virginia Woolf, or her one-time lover Vita Sackville-West; nor, indeed, to shift to a slightly different literary league, is she ever numbered among 'officially' acknowledged lesbian writers such as Natalie Barney or Radclyffe Hall. Still, Bowen's novels are often to be found on the 'lesbian fiction' shelves of women's and lesbian/gay bookstores, and to those who have developed a certain aptitude for reading from what I, current debates about the tenability of any such categorizing terms notwithstanding, would still prefer to call a lesbian perspective, Bowen's elusive and puzzling texts are indisputably part of a still not fully charted tradition of Western lesbian literature.[2]

Bowen pursued an active writing career for more than forty years. She published ten full-length novels, several collections of short stories, and an abundance of major and minor critical and other non-fictional works. All of her novels and a great many short stories would justify inclusion of the author in a book on cultural configurations of lesbian sexuality. I will nonetheless centre this chapter on a short novel written in the early 1930s, that is to say, at a time when some of the writers mentioned above (Woolf, Sackville-West, Hall and Barney), but also such diversely 'queer' figures as Gertrude Stein, H. D. (Henrietta Doolittle), Bryher, Margaret Anderson, and Renée Vivien – not to mention a host of less prominent, more recently rediscovered others – experienced fame, success and, as in some cases, disparagement and notoriety as the authors of texts that have, both at the time of publication and retroactively, been firmly placed within a lesbian context.[3] One reason why Bowen's name has not been incorporated in the still-expanding list of pre-war 'Sapphic' writers may be that she does not really seem to fit in: her work is difficult to classify, due to the elusive quality of its discursive style as much as its subject matter.[4] The novel singled out for discussion here, *Friends and Relations* (1931), is a case in point.[5] The very features that render any categorization of Bowen's fiction so problematical, however, can at the same time be seen to present a splendid illustration of some of the techniques and narrative strategies which allowed women writers of the first half of this century obliquely to textualize a distinctly lesbian desire.

Female authors of the 1930s tended to use divergent textual strategies and narrative techniques to give voice to their 'unspeakable' desires, hovering somewhere in between, on the one hand, the outspoken lesbian content and open articulation of a concomitantly 'perverse' desire articulated in novels and stories written since the Stonewall revolution, and, on the other, the sometimes densely codified, veiled representation of the 'love that dare not speak its name' in fiction originating in the (sexually repressive) period immediately following the Second World War. To adopt a provisional distinction of Shari Benstock's, one could say that there were those who 'followed traditional models of form and style, but whose subject matter was Sapphism', and others who 'filtered the lesbian content of their writing through the screen of presumably heterosexual subject matter or behind experimental literary styles'.[6] Elizabeth Bowen, I would argue, did both. In terms of subject matter and of overall narrative technique, her fiction is firmly grounded in a British tradition of social realism. Still, by equally partaking of the more experimental stylistic methods and disruptive narrative practices now largely associated with High Modernism, Bowen's writing at the same time radically transgresses the boundaries of any such neatly defined category. This deliberate fusion of what have since been recognized as discrete modes of literary expression has not only led to considerable confusion or, rather, critical dissent as to the author's place in literary history. My purpose in this chapter is to show that the 'unclassifiable' nature of Bowen's writing methods also offers the key to the disruptive sexual subtext underlying her dense and multi-layered narratives, which, on various interconnecting textual levels, attribute a critical role to the operations of female same-sex desire.

Friends and Relations, then, can be (re)appropriated as a lesbian text on several counts. First, and perhaps most straightforwardly, because of the incisive critique it presents of the established system of gender relations, by at once ruthlessly exposing its detrimental effects on individual characters' lives and, equally conspicuously, condemning the high costs of the compulsory enforcement of heteropatriarchal law in socio-ethical terms.[7] A second, related motive for such (re)appropriation would be the fact that the story's emotional and intellectual focus, despite an ostensible preoccupation with the problematical aspects of male/female relationships, indisputably lies with female same-sex interaction. Moreover, even though the actual word 'lesbian' occurs only once or twice in Bowen's texts (only in her later works, *The Little Girls* (1964) and *Eva Trout* (1969)), *Friends and Relations* forms no exception to the rest of her novels in featuring at least one explicitly lesbian character. In addition to these elements obtaining on a representational level, there is, however, a further aspect that most significantly and, I think, most effectively, inscribes the centrality of female same-sex desire in the text, that is, by making its presence felt on the novel's inter-twining patterns of narration and focalization. The joint and cumulative effects of these variously 'disruptive' sex/textual oper-ations will become clear in the course of my discussion. Let me, by way of introduction, first briefly dwell on Bowen's location in English social and literary history.

Friends and Relations was published in 1931. By that time, Elizabeth Bowen – who, in the words of her biographer Victoria Glendinning was 'heir, in literary and aesthetic terms, to Bloomsbury' – had already gained a small circle of admirers as the author of two novels and three volumes of short stories.[8] Although these early works had been fairly well received, it was only in the 1930s that the author acquired the prominence in the world of English letters that had been achieved a decade earlier by such notable figures as Virginia Woolf, E. M. Forster and Aldous Huxley. Bowen soon showed herself to be a most prolific writer: in the early years of the decade, her short stories started to appear in *The Listener*. She additionally began writing book reviews on a regular basis for the *New Statesman and Nation*, and, in 1936, by then an established novelist, wrote a first major essay for *The Spectator*. Bowen gained further recognition as the editor of *The Faber Book of Modern Short Stories*, a celebrated collec-tion which came out the same year as her essay on Jane Austen appeared in Derek Verschoyle's *The English Novelists*.[9] The nov-els for which this 'minor' author is, in some circles, still known today, were also written in the same period: *The House in Paris* met with wide critical acclaim in 1935, to be followed three years later by *The Death of the Heart*.[10]

If only because these years would turn out to be the most pro-ductive of her life, Bowen clearly earns her place within the gallery of other, recently rediscovered female writers of the 1930s, whose shared existence in the shadowy regions of early twentieth-century English literature is primarily due to the critical neglect they have suffered on account of their gender. Indeed, it is partly her status as a 'woman writer' that has landed Bowen, like so many female authors before and since, with a marginal place on the literary map. Starting with Jocelyn Brooke's short pamphlet of 1951, whose concluding note of praise highlights 'Miss Bowen's' prudence in not 'overstep[ping] the bounds' that come naturally with her sex, subsequent literary historians have, whether explicitly or implicitly, insisted on discussing her accomplishment in markedly gendered terms.[11] Where Brooke, in those blissful pre-feminist days, could still confidently identify the mere fact of her 'femininity' as the underlying cause of a 'self-imposed restriction' he attributes to Bowen's writing practice, later critics have gone some way to redress this gender-biased view on her achievement. Bowen's place in literary history generally, however, has continued to be defined in terms of restriction, alternately being traced to her class position or her gender identity – or, indeed, to both.

Douglas Hewitt, for example, numbers Bowen among those 'minor novelists' who 'established themselves in the late 1920s and 1930s', such as Ivy Compton-Burnett, Henry Green and Evelyn Waugh, whom he suggests to have 'chosen deliberately smaller subjects and to have turned their backs on technical innovation'.[12] Literally echoing Brooke, Hewitt remarks upon the 'self-imposed restrictions' these writers set themselves, the origins of which he locates not so much in the issue of gender as in that of class. Describing her narratives as 'limited' in 'social and emotional range', this mainstream literary historian's implicit gender bias makes itself felt when, without further ado, he classifies Bowen as a traditional novelist who published 'a number of delicate small-scale post Jamesian studies, mostly of children and adolescent girls'.[13]

A self-professed feminist critic such as Rosalind Miles, whose stated purpose it is to counter the 'extraordinary process of denial and annihilation' that persists in negating the 'supremacy of the role of women writers in the evolution of the modern novel', reinforces rather than redresses such standard practices of sexual stereotyping when briefly discussing Bowen. Isolating hers as a 'classic case' among forgotten 'women writers whose reputations in their own day were not merely respectable but towering', Miles nonetheless repeats precisely the kind of constraining gestures which she purports to denounce, though ostensibly reiterating

Hewitt's emphasis on class rather than sex. Reducing Bowen's 'gift' to the 'evocation of class romance', she rejects what she mis-reads as 'unexamined social assumptions' which, and here sex obliquely re-enters the discussion, also underlie the work of Rosamond Lehmann, 'though [the latter's] subject matter and technique are not otherwise comparable with those of Elizabeth Bowen'.[14] Unfortunately, the differences between these two authors (whose names often appear associated) remain unspeci-fied, so that we never learn why Bowen's 'towering' reputation suffered so much more seriously from the process of critical malestreaming than Lehmann's – or, for that matter, those of other 'minor' women novelists – are implied to have done.

Even fairly recent accounts of twentieth-century literary his-tory thus prolong the impression that Bowen was a class-conscious, if not snobbish writer of sensibility, whose work, due to the mutually reinforcing constraints of both her class and her sex, is narrow in scope, romantic and technically conventional. The question of sexuality, or the potentially sexual nature of the 'partiality' structuring her fictions' eccentric perspectives, does not enter into these discussions at all.

In apparent contrast, two on the whole appreciative critics of Bowen's, Hermione Lee and Victoria Glendinning, dare indeed mention the sensitive lesbian subject, but only in order vehe-mently to deny its relevance to either the author's life or her work.[15] Such reluctance to acknowledge the centrality of the 'unspeakable' topic is all the more a pity, since a recognition of the unsettling, sexually ambiguous subtexts underpinning Bowen's narratives might, as I have argued elsewhere, have enabled them to shed considerable light on previous critics' ges-tures of adverse praise in the overdetermined, belittling terms of 'smallness' and 'narrowness'.[16] In their attempts to prevent Bowen's reputation from becoming even more tainted than it apparently already is, this time by what undoubtedly counts as the most stigmatizing label of all, that is, the suggestion of a 'les-bian sensibility', critics such as Lee and Glendinning do not sim-ply reinforce the process of 'denial and annihilation' that has (even more powerfully and persistently than the 'role of women writers in the evolution of the modern novel') traditionally befallen the lesbian subject in mainstream literary criticism and historiography. Precisely by taking great pains to repudiate any past or potential 'accusations' of lesbianism, they also, though perhaps inadvertently, render all too obvious the decidedly 'queer' aspects to Bowen's writing that – however 'unfortunate' this may appear to these self-appointed guardians of the author's good name – cannot be simply overlooked by any serious reader of her work. In other words, such impassioned assertions to the contrary indicate that there is incontrovertible evidence in the story of the author's life as well as her work that attests to the operation of lesbian desire: only its tangible presence would seem to be capable of calling forth the need for such strenuous disavowal.

Both here and in my earlier work on Bowen, it has been my purpose to explore those features that have consistently been suggested to 'weaken' her fiction, the very idiosyncrasies that have led to her marginalization in both masculist and feminist practices of literary historiography.[17] What is frequently denounced as a particularly delimiting aspect of her narrative methods, that is to say, the conspicuous partiality of, in Hewitt's words, the 'rather unusual points of view' shaping her texts, I consider not so much a flaw marking even the best of her fiction but, instead, a manifestation of the author's unorthodox intellectual and emotional take on the world. Bowen's peculiar viewpoints signal a deliberate refusal to aspire to – as literary convention would have it – a 'general', or even 'universal' perspective.[18] Precisely the presumed 'queerness' in terms of narrative scope testifies to an acute awareness of the 'situatedness' of Bowen's speaking/writing self, that is, of her shifting yet irretrievably gendered, sexualized and class-bound position in society, and, by extension, to her conscious recognition of the profoundly determined/determining ways in which such socio-symbolic locations are inevitably, both consciously and unconsciously, projected onto her fictions. Signalling the spuriousness of any individual's claim to what even today, in our multicultural times, tends to pass for a 'general' point of view, it is this 'unusual' degree of self-awareness that informs the radical, if not subversive potential of Bowen's work.[19] What is more, the operations of her sharp insight into the necessarily implicated nature of her own or, for that matter, any individual's, position in the socio-symbolic order, predominantly find expression in an outspoken sex/textual ambiguity. It is, in effect, in this discursive realm that the destabilizing effects of Bowen's 'rather unusual points of view' become most palpable.

Friends and Relations is an evasive text.[20] Its style is dense and elaborate, the narrative tone of voice amused yet non-committal, while the narrative as a whole is qualified by a sustained sense of negativity, which is only occasionally relieved by vivid patches of social comedy. The mere 150-odd pages of this shortest of Bowen's novels fall into three parts, all more or less equal in length. To discuss *Friends and Relations* in terms of plot development would be slightly beside the point, for the novel contains little or no plot to speak of. The whole of its dramatic impact derives from what is, as one of the characters correctly observes, no more than a 'large non-occurrence' (151). Since it is obviously not the narrative events themselves – such as they are – that are central to its signifying operations, it appears all the more appropriate to concentrate on the ways in which the text takes shape and acquires meaning through the complexities in narrative perspective, especially since the mediating look of the authorial narrator is supplemented with several other focalizing instances.[21]

Friends and Relations opens in the Malvern hills near Cheltenham, at some time during the 1920s. At Corunna Lodge, the rural abode of a retired Army officer and his wife, we meet the story's heroines, Laurel and Janet Studdart. At once evoking and inverting a tradition that goes back as far as the English novel proper, the narrative begins where romantic fiction usually ends: under the 'inauspicious mutter' of steadily falling rain, the stage is being set for the wedding of the elder daughter, Laurel, to handsome Edward Tilney. Under the mildly ironic gaze of the authorial narrator, the Studdarts, nervously giving 'instructions' and looking after 'arrangements', reveal their preoccupation with social decorum, their anxiety to abide by the rules of country propriety. The comic depiction of the theatricalities involved in this most admirable of social occasions initiates a line of narrative critique which is sustained throughout. But while providing the perfect scene for the effective exposure of the moral inertia reigning within this pleasant middle-class family, the wedding also yields the germs of what Bowen has called the 'internal combustion' on which the movement of plot depends.[22]

That things are not all as happy as they may seem becomes clear when the text obliquely discloses that morose-looking Janet secretly desires her sister's highly-strung fiancé, whose 'dazzling courtship of the entire family' in the preceding months had not for some time 'particularized in the direction of Laurel' (16). With Edward serving as a yardstick, an apparent contrast is set up between the two sisters: the groom's emotional balance eventually tipped in favour of Laurel's fairness, charm and 'irregular prettiness', at the expense of her younger sister, who has 'little charm', appearing 'even forbidding' (14; 15). The more elusive character of the two, the dark, 'heavy-lidded and rather sombre Diana' is compensated for her lack of womanly charm by seeming more 'interesting'. Whether she is as potentially tragic a figure as may at first appear remains unclear, however, for the author-narrator's sympathies seem evenly divided: Janet is as much a target of subtle but stinging irony as her more successfully 'feminine' sibling. Being prematurely ousted from the romantic plot, the younger Studdart additionally figures as an object of pity among the assembled wedding guests. Yet, as one of them sensibly reflects: 'Girls could not all expect to marry' (13), and Janet, fortunately, has 'many interests', presently being occupied with supervising her Wolf Cubs.

While the attractive bridal pair ostensibly draw all our attention, it is the bridegroom's mother, Lady Elfrida – 'always a little too gracefully [playing] a losing game' – who stands at the uneasy centre of the narrative scene. 'Being a *divorcée* (a circumstance which, the narrator comments, 'should but does not subdue'), this figure 'in claret-coloured georgette', it transpires, forms a potential threat to the ritual establishment of the Studdart/Tilney connection presently being enacted (10). Having left Edward's father some twenty years earlier for one-time explorer and big-game hunter Considine Meggatt, Lady Elfrida had not only failed to do the proper thing, that is, marry her 'co-respondent', but also disdained the most consecrated of her womanly tasks, abandoning her child to the care of assorted relatives, while making her way to Paris to work her way through the war in a hospital in the South of France. Such sexual, social and moral independence in a woman of her position obviously does not sit comfortably with either the gender conventions or the class codes by which the middle-class system of friends and relations sustains itself. Showing the boundaries between these two axes of exclusion – gender and class – to be so intricately entwined as to become almost indistinguishable, the Studdarts, not knowing 'whether to condemn her as a lady or as a woman', consider their extravagant new relative an altogether distressing social liability (17).

Slightly off-centre amidst the main cast of characters, Lady Elfrida is in an excellent position to focus the novel's central lines of class and gender critique. Her private thoughts about the Studdart sisters are particularly effective in reinforcing the implied contrast between them. Whilst not subscribing to her new relatives' ambition to keep up the 'happy tradition' of girls' marrying 'out of [their] 'teens', Lady Elfrida would have preferred to see her son's difficult character being entrusted to the capable hands of the younger of the Studdart sisters. Perceiving Laurel's motherly concern with his 'surviving childish gravity', she correctly anticipates the bride's future indulgence of Edward's ruthless egotism (15). Such regret on the part of this formidable female figure does not stem from her own maternal anxieties. Rather, precisely because she is socially cast in the role of 'disreputable mother', Lady Elfrida knows what ravaging effects female complicity with established gender convention may have, especially on members of her sex who choose not to comply with the rules. It is, after all, precisely such accommodating girls as her lovely daughter-in-law who unwittingly uphold the double standard by which she herself still cannot but be regarded as *declassée*. And, since it is possible to defy, but not to live outside, the rules of social convention, the sight of Laurel's soothing response to Edward's 'perversity' and 'impassibility', evokes, in 'less than [a] moment of consternation', the feeling that 'her own life was ruined, ruined – ' (14).

Though generally unrepentant, Lady Elfrida has paid for her independence with a life of 'few friends, near solitude'. The odd one out among the older generation, she at once takes a liking to Janet, whose relative exclusion from the wedding scene equally seems to reduce her stakes in middle-class pretension. When, therefore, barely six weeks later, her new friend announces her engagement to Rodney Meggatt – nephew to Lady Elfrida's own one-time 'co-respondent' Considine – the news cannot but strike Lady Elfrida as a 'personal disappointment' (18).

As my reading of the opening scene so far suggests, *Friends and Relations'* thematic focus falls unequivocally on the operation of patriarchal gender ideology in society generally, and within the confines of the traditional middle-class family in particular. It may at first seem far-fetched to read such an outspoken critique of the dominant gender system in a novel whose drama is so emphatically 'underplayed', and whose finely attuned texture creates a highly-wrought atmosphere of overall indirection. We should bear in mind, however, that at the time of its writing the 'Woman Question' had come to figure centrally on the English social stage. By the end of the 1920s, the heyday of the first feminist wave, with its heated parliamentary debates and public outrage over suffragette militancy, had long been over. But the radical socio-cultural changes of the *fin-de-siècle*, and the subsequent decline of the Victorian family and its values, had given rise to a general sense of despair at the crumbling of the Old Order, which, in retrospect, to many seemed to have coincided with the emergence of the early women's liberation movement. Moreover, in the aftermath of the Great War (to which women from all walks of life had actively contributed), many middle-class women refused to resume their former roles as Angels in the House. This furthered in the public mind the connection between the gloomy, even apocalyptic visions of the future of civilization – articulated, for example, in T. S. Eliot's *The Waste Land* (1922) – and the changes that had irreversibly altered relations between the sexes, both in society at large and in the middle-class family home.[23] The text obliquely alludes to these larger socio-historical questions when we learn that Rodney has been raised on his uncle Considine's 'cheerful ruthless generalizations as to the Sex'. While suggesting the lingering centrality of the Woman Question in social discourse, this remark simultaneously serves further to inscribe the differences between Janet and Laurel, which, ironically, find most pronounced expression in the characters of their respective husbands. Whereas handsome young Edward and his pretty new bride appear to represent the perfect couple, both Janet and Rodney are suggested to take up exceptional positions within the fiction of heterosexual romance. In contrast to his brother-in-law's near-indistinct appetite for female charm, 'the Sex', we are informed, 'did not interest [Rodney]'. His attraction to his future wife stems instead from the sombre 'Diana' 's 'rather masculine unawareness of "situation"'(37).

In addition to highlighting the interactive and interdependent operations of the exclusionary processes of socio-cultural differentiation – here jointly focused on the categories of class, age and gender – the most significant fact about the wedding scene, at least within the context of the present discussion, is that the author-narrator's is not the only perspective we gain on this festive occasion. While the latter's wry comments sharply call into question the oppressive operations of patriarchal gender ideology, we are offered an outspokenly sexual perspective on the scene by a precocious fifteen-year-old girl, Theodora Thirdman, whose vivid mental observations punctuate the static character of the entire sequence.

As one of her favourite character-types to explore questions of sexual desire and identity, the figure of the female adolescent functions as an ambivalent yet privileged signifier in Bowen's fiction generally.[24] If not on account of her conspicuously alliterative and highly suggestive name, Theodora hence immediately draws our attention. 'Awkwardly anxious to make an impression', the girl's striking looks and snide remarks (which result in her being altogether ignored) unwittingly remind the assorted company of their tenuous hold on their own socio-cultural positions. But it is not only the female adolescent's value as a transitional figure in the growth to gendered adulthood that makes Theodora's a disturbing presence. Explicitly identified as a 'third man', at a moment in history when concepts such as the 'Third Sex', the 'mannish lesbian' and the female 'invert' were no longer restricted to professional sexological discourse only, but were, in fact, becoming widely familiar to the public at large, Theodora first and foremost occupies a potentially subversive position with regard to the heterosexual imperative, which, receiving its official stamp at occasions like these, forms the underlying focus of the narrator's scornful gaze.

The centrality of the question of 'perverse' female desire, that is 'perverse', in the sense of not being oriented towards heterosexual reproduction, is stressed by the fact that almost half of the opening scene is filtered through the mind of this sexually ambiguous figure, the 'spectacled, large-boned', and unengaging female adolescent. Significantly, it is our glimpse into the inner landscape of this literal bystander which allows us to become aware of Janet's suppressed passion for her brother-in-law. Realizing that this 'was a day of chagrin, possibly of despair' for her, Theodora develops an instant attraction for the 'masculine' younger Studdart – attraction, not love, the narrator adds, for due to her 'unfortunate age', the girl 'could understand, but not yet love'(13). Despite the authorial 'overlordship' this and other such comments express, Theodora's curious vision on characters and events is not so much secondary to as virtually parallel to the narrator's. While certainly not exempt from the latter's superior irony, the gawky adolescent's astute observations thus substantially qualify the author-narrator's seemingly omnipotent, organizing look. Through this strategy of double focalization, the text not only challenges the notion of a 'general' perspective, but, indirectly yet unmistakably, also gives voice to the 'unspeakable' sexual subtext that underlies its overtly articulated gender critique.

Theodora's mental observations provide us with the view of a socio-sexual outsider on traditional female lives geared to 'romantic love', the constraining effects of which are shown to find their formal seal in its institutional enactment: the joining of man and woman in holy matrimony. Belying her name by occupying a privileged position on the novel's extradiegetic level, the 'godsent' creature will, we shall see in a moment, additionally play a subversive role in the all but dramatic plot, by threatening to throw into confusion the static play that is being enacted on the text's representational, or intradiegetic, level.

In the remaining pages of the novel's first section, Theodora's story and those of the principal heroines continue to run side by side, occasionally intersecting each other. While the young Studdarts face up to what their respective transfers from one man's hands to those of another will entail, Theodora seeks refuge from her well-meaning but 'absolutely *superfluous*' parents (28) to attend a girls' boarding school in Surrey. Enjoying the 'excellence of [a] Swiss education', there is little for her extraordinary brain to gain in terms of formal knowledge. However, since the girls at Mellyfield are primarily 'interested in their own personalities, which they displayed, discussed and altered', Theodora, already having 'a good deal of personality' at her disposal, succeeds in causing a pleasurable disturbance and distinguishes herself by 'making a marvellous man' in the school's Saturday night plays (28; 44).

Beginning with Elaine Marks' influential essay 'Lesbian Intertextuality' (1979),[25] critics and historians of lesbian literature have been united in singling out the girls' school as one of the most powerful and consistently employed mimetic contexts in which, as Terry Castle recently put it, 'plots of lesbian desire are likely to flourish'.[26] The origin of what in the eighteenth century became a full-fledged lesbian *topos*, the chronotope of the girls' school as a potential site of same-sex eroticism, is usually traced back to the myth of the Greek poet Sappho, who reputedly initiated the young girls sent to her for the finishing touch to their polite education, in more than what later eras would consider 'proper' female accomplishments. As is suggested by the contemporary meanings reverberating through both the name of the poet and that of the idyllic island of Lesbos on which her 'gynaeceum' was located, the Sapphic myth centres on same-sexual activities that were supposed to prepare the young females entrusted to the poet's cultivating hands for their future roles as wives and mothers.

The story of Lesbos has continued to function as an enabling imaginary space in fictional texts throughout the eighteenth, nineteenth, and well into the twentieth centuries, developing into a discursive realm in which the otherwise taboo subject of lesbianism could be culturally represented and explored.[27] But whilst the Sappho-model may have partly served to give shape and direction to the development of a specifically lesbian literary tradition, it has simultaneously functioned as an effective ideological mould by means of which lesbian sexuality could be confined to a separate cultural sphere, to be contained within an all-female environment safely out of the real world. Relegated to the mythical realm of fairy tale and romance, or, conversely, to the equally mythical transitional realm of pre-adulthood, female same-sex desire has traditionally been split off from both social reality and, just as effectively, from the sexual arena dominating the collective imagination, that is, gendered heterosexuality.

That Bowen deliberately exploits these various markers of lesbian desire is underlined when Theodora, upon learning that Janet's engagement is momentarily called off, 'c[an]not help thinking, "This may be where I come in?"'(45). This, of course, is not to be, for even if Edward's being 'difficult' about the inconvenient family connection the younger Studdart's marriage would set up between himself and Considine causes the engagement to be for one day suspended, the whole 'miserable affair' proves not sufficiently inconvenient as to put the 'scandalous' Meggatt-Tilney alliance on the line. Reinscribing the cultural value of adolescence as a preliminary or transitional stage, the narrative focus from that moment onwards rests primarily with the newly established, extended network of 'adult', that is to say, heterosexual friends and relations.

Significantly, when the vicissitudes of the adolescent's 'theatrical' life gradually fade into the background to allow for the uneventful main plot further to unfold, the novel loses much of both its comic and its narrative momentum. The function of the adolescent character in *Friends and Relations* therewith proves to be not dissimilar to that of another of Bowen's unruly heroines, the young girl Portia, appearing in *The Death of the Heart* (1938), about whom the author said in an interview in 1950:

> I've heard [*The Death of the Heart*] . . . called a tragedy of adolescence. I never thought of it that way when I wrote it and I must say I still don't see it in that way now. The one adolescent character in it, the young girl Portia seems to me to be less tragic than the others. She at least, has a hope, and she hasn't atrophied. The book really is a study, it might be presumptuous of me to call it a tragedy of atrophy, not of death so much as of death sleep. And the function of Portia in the story is to be the awake one, in a sense therefore she was a required character. She imparts meaning rather than carries meaning.[28]

As the 'awake one' among an equally spiritually and emotionally 'atrophied' cast of characters as the ones figuring in this later novel, Theodora, literally a gift of the gods, may be temporarily confined to the narrative backstage, but she continues to 'impart' the rather grim meanings of the story unravelling in its front. The full extent of her revitalizing powers will reveal themselves shortly.

Having momentarily left Theodora to perfect her personality at Mellyfield, the narrator pursues her study of 'atrophied' family life by disclosing the background to Janet's acceptance of Rodney. The younger Studdart's decision to marry Considine's nephew, we learn, was inspired by her wish to be officially related to Edward: though separate they would be linked by scandal. The narrator leaves no doubt as to the moral failure this concession to middle-class convention represents. By becoming a wife and mother, and thus blending into the social network, Janet wilfully succumbs to the stultifying power of 'ordinary' family life. Abandoning her claim to subjective agency, and thus reinforcing the operation of an oppressive system of unequal gender relations, her failure to live up to her suggested potential – the ultimate character flaw in Bowen's ethical framework – is not merely a sign of personal deficiency: it signifies first and foremost a foregoing of one's social responsibility. But, as Janet herself is later astutely to point out, this is, after all, precisely what families are all about: 'It's possible to be so ordinary; it's possible not to say such a lot' (49; 47).

Foregrounding the novel's overall line of gender critique, the section's concluding note reinserts Theodora firmly at the centre of the text's moral vision. Once again, this occurs in an indirect way, this time by means of an implicit yet striking comparison between her unorthodox personality and those of the two girls at the forefront of the narrative stage. In spite of their overt dissimilarities in character, Janet, with her dark, brooding nature, and Laurel, always excelling in pleasant superficiality, are exposed to inevitable and similar moulding by the gendered grid of middle-class convention. It falls to Lady Elfrida to articulate the precise import of this revelation. Seemingly unaccountably, at some point she expresses regret at Janet's having had a sister at all, hitting on an unexpected truth when she subsequently observes: '"I always feel, with women, the mould should have been broken, not used again and again"'(38). Whereas the confining female 'mould' evidently has not been broken within the Studdart family, Theodora, in contrast, being both an only child and manifestly an incongruous third party in the cycle of feminine duplication, stands out as the embodiment of unconventional female subjectivity. She therewith not only merits the narrator's (and the reader's) primary interest, but also obtains significance on an extra-textual and socio-ethical level. The curious figure's value as 'privileged signifier' on the novel's moral plane is underscored by the ideas Bowen voiced elsewhere on the distinction between fictional and non-fictional characters:

> As a novelist, I cannot not occupy myself with 'characters', or at any rate central ones, who lack panache in one or another sense, who would be incapable of a major action or a major passion, or who have not at least a touch of the ambiguity, the ultimate unaccountability, the enlarging mystiness of personages 'in history'.[29]

Despite evidence to the contrary, it is not therefore, as previous critics have claimed, Janet's repressed feelings for Edward that stand at the centre, while simultaneously posing a threat to, the gendered class system the novel holds up for critical scrutiny. Rather, as my foregoing comments seek to convey, it is the *extra*-ordinary presence of Theodora Thirdman in the margins of the interlocking heterosexual plots which constitutes the story's undercurrent disruptive force. Moreover, as we have seen, the odd figure is not only a potentially subversive presence within the established gender system depicted on the novel's representational level. In her critical function as the second-most important focalizing instance, the adolescent character also undercuts the narrator's authority in imparting the story's underlying sexual meanings. By moving centre-stage in the novel's middle, indeed, central section, in order additionally to assume the role of interruptive narrative agent, the female 'third man' conclusively inscribes her significance as the text's ideological and inner moral core.

Entitled 'The Fine Week', Part Two takes us ten years ahead in time. We meet Janet and Rodney living a quietly rural life with their daughter Hermione at the Meggatt estate annex fruit farm, Batts Abbey, whilst Laurel and Edward share a more sociable existence with their two children in London's Royal Avenue. The scene is Batts, where both the young Tilneys, Edward's best man Lewis Gibson, Colonel Studdart, and Considine have joined the

Meggatts to spend this fine week in midsummer. Conspicuously absent is Lady Elfrida, whose visits have hitherto not been allowed to coincide with those of both Considine and Edward's children, since their father is still being 'difficult' about the scandalous family connection. That something is about to disturb the placid surface of this exemplary scene of family life is intimated when Janet and Rodney suddenly decide to break with their long-standing practice of enforced delicacy. The narrator comments:

> Today proved to be one of those weekdays, vacant, utterly without character, when some moral fort of a lifetime is abandoned calmly, almost idly, without the slightest assault from circumstance. So religions are changed, celibacy relinquished, marriages broken up, or there occurs a first large breach with personal honour. (69)

The relevance of these rather portentous remarks does not immediately become clear, for the decision to invite Janet's old friend Lady Elfrida to join the party does not evoke any response from Edward. Laurel, in contrast, lets her sister know that she does 'not feel so much as though there had been an earthquake, but as though I should never see you, or you would be different' (70). Lady Elfrida's prompt arrival does, indeed, occasion little disturbance. It is only a few days later, when Theodora Thirdman pays tribute to her first name by descending upon the scene in the role of a proper *deus ex machina*, that the narrator's comments and Laurel's sense of foreboding begin to acquire more definite meaning.

By now in her mid-twenties, Theodora has grown into a handsome professional woman, sharing a fashionable London attic flat with a former schoolmate who, significantly, earns her living as a creative writer. Since the formerly so unsettling power of Lady Elfrida's unconventional personality has obviously diminished – the joint presence of the elderly 'sinners' has left the quiet family scene virtually unruffled – the way is cleared for the disruptive potential of the unorthodox figure of Theodora Thirdman to come to the narrative surface. Displacing the disreputable mother from her accustomed position as *agent provocateur* within the middle-class network of friends and relations, it is she who presently upsets the 'delicate rhythm' of the smoothly running family machinery.

Theodora's unexpected visit to Batts affects the individual family members as much as it produces a disconcerting effect on the party as a whole. Lady Elfrida, for one, usually quite capable of cunningly exploiting her feminine charm, admits to feeling 'quite hysterical' in the presence of what she quickly perceives to be a 'dark horse' in the heterosexual family realm. In an attempt to subdue the anxiety provoked by the daunting 'masculine' creature, she at once acknowledges and dismisses the nature of Theodora's oddness: 'She had passions for women – awkward, such a tax on behaviour, like nausea at meals' (82).[30] Even Janet, who has made it her life's work to perfect her role as a 'positive no-presence' (33), inadvertently allows her guest to stir up memories of that 'extinct sin' that accounts for the 'persistence of an emotional Edward in [her] landscape' (77). Indulging Theodora's open expression of fondness for her, the connection between her intrusive visitor and her brother-in-law – in their shared function as Hermione's godparents – releases the repressed desires from the 'old crater, now so cheerfully verdant' of her inner landscape. As if waking up from a dream, Janet soon finds herself silently reiterating that she 'still lived and had to command emotion' (74).

Theodora still harbours her 'adolescent' desires for Janet, and cannot refrain from openly displaying a 'lucid perplexity' as to the capable housewife's uneventful and orderly life. The independent young woman blames Edward for the moral and spiritual atrophy she perceives in the object of her desires, and cannot forgive him the tenure he has, 'this mortmain on Janet's spirit'. Despite the fact that the 'whole theory of victimization' is disagreeable to her, Theodora therefore decides that it is 'time *something* happened' (77; 75). Intent upon breaking through the undintable surface of Janet's orderly life, she secretly sends off a letter to Laurel. With this mysterious missive, she succeeds in bringing Edward storming down on Batts, supposedly to rescue his children from the corrupt company of the sinful old couple – almost a week after Lady Elfrida's arrival. That his passionate outrage stems from another source, rather than from any professed concern for his children's spiritual welfare, is obliquely revealed when we finally get to read the letter that has brought Edward down in a fury. Not only does it contain hints about the Meggatts' 'unreciprocal' love, it also suggests 'unspeakable' goings-on between its concipient and the lady of the house. While innocent enough in themselves ('I brush her hair at nights; I brush well. Never let her cut it'), such intimations of female same-sex interaction have aroused Edward's almost congenital jealousy. Janet is obviously right when she perceptively remarks: '*You* can't bear anything to be going on that you're not in. You behave like someone who's missed a train' (94).

Theodora's intervention has been successful insofar as it has produced a crack in the surface of Janet's sealed-off existence. The confrontation with Edward's passionate outrage has, in fact, landed the self-contained housewife on the verge of a nervous breakdown. Still, the emotional turmoil in its mistress produces no more than the semblance of a crisis which, remaining unarticulated, continues to spread in barely acknowledged ripples through the house. Theodora and the young Hermione manifestly enjoy the subdued commotion, while Rodney merely notes a sudden cleft between him and his wife, whose silent rebuff he accepts without resentment. Edward, not surprisingly, is equally shown incapable of rising to the occasion: weighing the balance between Janet and Laurel, he realizes that the latter's solicitude, reaching him 'almost before he suffered, fostering sensibility', is something he cannot do without: 'Life after all,' he observes, 'is an affair of charm, not an affair of passion' (99). Even Lady Elfrida, suffering a solitary moment of guilt when confronted with her son's being so 'miserably hard', shies away from the unsettling situation. 'Impatient for herself and her sex,' she swiftly disassociates herself from the whole affair, implying that 'it's impossible to be anything but indifferent' (102). Whereas Lady Elfrida is, on the whole, treated with marked narrative sympathy, such a wilful act of indifference on the part of this exceptional female character is unequivocally condemned on moral grounds. Though not exempt from narrative critique, the concluding pages of the novel's middle section nonetheless show how both Lady Elfrida's and to a lesser extent, Janet's moral fallibility are primarily the result of the gendered operations of a stultifying class system.

A nocturnal conversation between the two friends brings the moral implications of the novel's social critique unambiguously to the fore. Under Lady Elfrida's close observation, Janet looks back on the past to gain a perspective on her bewildering present. 'With passive docility', she explains that, after what had been a 'false dawn' to her, that is, falling in love with Edward, she had felt at a loss: '"No one explained the part to me. So I stood there with no words to say and nothing to do with my hands"' (106). Offered a place in the heteropatriarchal network of friends and relations, she had allowed Rodney to give her life's directions. But in 'lend[ing] herself to retrospect', Janet comes dangerously close to understanding the fragility of the family structure in which she believes to have found firm foothold. The narrator/focalizer merges with the character's consciousness to unfold a complex pattern of imagery.

Through Janet's mind's eye we perceive the image of a tree, 'fatal apple-tree in a stained-glass window' which, rooted in that 'old branching sin', hides in its shadows Considine and Elfrida, 'related only in balance for the design'. The tree of carnal knowledge/sin gradually turns into the tree of Jesse – 'that springing – not, you would think, without pain somewhere, from a human side', in which, Janet realizes, one 'vital incision' would be enough to bring all those 'perplexed similar faces' tumbling down, to be scattered about like July apples, having 'no more part in each other at all'. The narrator's asides reveal that it is her friend Lady Elfrida who has suffered the pain for the flowering of this illusory structure: now so 'impatient of all this burden', she has paid for her independence by being forever in the wrong: '"Never to be in the right – it's the only possible ruin, I daresay, if one's nothing besides a woman"' (104; 107).

Apart from spelling out the import of the novel's central line of social critique, the sequence further exposes the moral deficiency of its once most promising female hero. Burning out her intent look on Janet's downcast eyes, Lady Elfrida, who had hoped much of 'any break with the amenities', is forced to accept that nothing is going to happen after all: her young friend's emotional detachment merely 'made her enigmatic when indeed she was not enigmatic at all but a plain woman' (109). Ready for 'the call, any call', Janet subsequently makes her escape by, significantly, attending to Hermione's night fears, happy that she can 'presently . . . creep away' (110).

In the opening scenes of the novel's final section, 'Wednesday', it momentarily seems as if Janet will, after all, succeed in breaking 'with the amenities' by giving herself over to the 'high kind of overruling disorder' called love (109). Edward, however, though briefly tempted to flatter his ego by giving in to his attraction to his 'interesting' sister-in-law, at the last moment balks at the 'inconvenient cruelty of passion' (119). Whereas he does suggest that they might 'comfort each other', his moral and emotional depravation renders him incapable of facing up to Janet's 'passionate fatality' (128). At the end of the day, Edward once again seeks refuge in the 'miniature happiness' offered by his wife's ever-comforting arms, while Janet returns to the indestructible safety of Batts Abbey (105).

What could have been a devastating family tragedy thus amounts to what is, as mentioned before, no more than a 'large non-occurrence'. The disruptive script of genuine passion, its power to shatter 'all the dear conventions', ultimately appears to have no effect on any of the players figuring frontstage in the family romance. Only in the minds of those figures in the background – eternal bystander Lewis Gibson and 'queer Theodora' (155) – who have no role to play in the heterosexual gender scenario to begin with, does the unsettling force of emotion amount to something with reality-value. When, for a moment, it seems as if Edward and Janet have run away together, these onlookers meet on their common ground in the margins of the dominant socio-cultural plot.

Lewis's apparent consternation nonetheless soon turns out to be basically a rather selfish chagrin. Feeling ousted from his position as friend of the family, he reproachfully observes: '"They've got their cue, but they're leaving all of us none"' (145). 'Dramatic in her sincere misery', Theodora is the only character with the moral courage to break with the bland civilities of 'happy custom', in order unrestrainedly to express her feelings. At once furious, jealous and truly unhappy, she bursts out: '"I can't stand this; I love her! I tell you, idiot, I love her beyond propriety – "' (146). 'Land-bound' Lewis, seriously taken aback by such unwonted emotional energy, can merely icily admit that, 'Yes, it is most upsetting' (146).

Bringing the story-line full circle, the novel's closing paragraphs take us back to Corunna Lodge. The narrator's gloss on the

Studdart daughters' yearly visits to their parental home, the 'family reconstruct[ing] itself with talk and laughter', at first seems to convey a sense of happy restoration. The poignant irony, however, which qualifies the depiction of Cheltenham civilization effects a merciless exposure of its inhabitants' moral complacency and spiritual atrophy. Mrs Studdart's guilt-ridden yet discriminating thoughts concerning her daughters' impaled lives and defective personalities further underline the destructive consequences of the fact that the near-immutable, ideologically enforced heterosexual gender 'mould' has, in the end, not been broken.

The main beneficiaries of the restoration of order, the reassertion of the power of the family, are the nominal heroes of the novel's first section: Edward, once more indulging in his wife's unfailing maternal forgiveness, and Rodney, passively acquiescent, content to have Janet back, even if she 'had explained nothing, accounted for nothing' (135). Their wives, in contrast, are shown to have sustained substantial losses as a result of the socially reassuring outcome of recent (non)-events. For one thing, their sisterly bond has been sorely affected: although the 'catastrophe [had been] very quiet' (129), an irreparable cleft has been wrought between them. Laurel's feelings for Edward have furthermore lost their youthful ingenuousness: she warily foresees a 'hundred solitary woman's wakings, beside but without him' (153). Neither of the female characters are cast as mere 'victims' of the heterosexual gender system, despite the fact that the benefits reaped from the restoration of family stability are obviously unequally divided along gendered lines. Laurel, it is suggested, consciously reassumes a position of complicity within the established power–gender relations by seeking refuge in that age-old feminine strategy, leaving things unsaid. Realizing that it is only by 'keep[ing] still, not rocking their boat' that she and Edward will be able to continue 'along the smooth stream', she wilfully seeks oblivion (153). If the older sister's social and moral cowardice is denounced in mildly critical terms, Janet's resumption of her longstanding practice of spiritual and emotional self-mutilation is brought to the fore more poignantly. Having decided that it is her life's purpose to entomb herself in 'thought that was no thought', the once-passionate Diana wakes up the day after her nocturnal non-adventures in London to take charge of the annual meeting of 'the Mother's Union', taking place on the lawn of her patrilinearly-acquired home.

The condemnatory tone of the narrative voice in these final paragraphs indirectly underscores the point that only the figure of Theodora Thirdman, though all but fading into the background, can ultimately stand up to moral scrutiny. As the only truly 'awake one', the queer godsend/*agent provocateur* functions both literally and symbolically as the focal point of the novel's overarching ethical framework. Indeed, as Bowen has repeatedly pointed out, it is 'sensationalists' like Theodora who form the privileged signifiers in the typical 'Bowen terrain':

> Bowen characters are in transit *consciously*. Sensationalists, they are able to re-experience what they do, or equally, what is done to them, every day. They tend to behold afresh and react accordingly.[31]

Considering Bowen's own career as a writer and critic, it should come as no surprise that it is a professional, independent young woman who should come to perform this pivotal function in a novel which critically addresses the intertwining operations of oppressive class and gender systems. However, the character in question embodies more than a foible to offset the culturally constraining and emotionally impoverishing effects of dominant power-gender relations. Apart from her outspokenly 'deviant' role within the pervasively heterocentrist socio-symbolic order against which the narrative is set, Theodora Thirdman also performs a pivotal role as the principal conveyor of the text's underlying sexual meanings. It is, in effect, on account of her privileged position on the discursive, or extradiegetic, level of the text that the ex-centric figure acquires most pointed significance as a radically disruptive sex/textual force. Although inevitably subordinated to the narrator's eventually prevailing orchestrating powers, the female 'third man' hence allows for the unauthorized voice of 'perverse' desire to speak through, with, and against the authorial discourse of the primary narrative agent.

That it should fall to a 'female invert' to become the principal mediating focus in not just this, but in a substantial number of Bowen's other fictions as well, does perhaps no more than illustrate that even a highly self-conscious writer such as Bowen will, to recall the quote framing this chapter, 'like a swimmer caught by an undertow', inevitably be 'borne in an unexpected direction.... captured by some experience to which one may have hardly given a thought'. If there is one defining feature that could capture the quality of Bowen's variegated writing practice, it would be precisely such willingness to be lured by the unknown and the unexpected, both to embrace and articulate experience in all of its destabilizing aspects. The resulting idiosyncrasies qualifying her novelistic discourse have no doubt played a considerable part in rendering her sometimes disconcertingly ambivalent fictions liable to all sorts of misappropriation. But these selfsame qualities of evasiveness and ambiguity also allow for further appropriations, as, for instance, exemplified by the interested kind of reading that I have tried to perform in the preceding pages. And even though it would clearly be inappropriate to categorize Bowen as a 'lesbian' author in the contemporary sense of the term, it is, in the final instance, these very undefinable and unclassifiable sex/textual aspects that both invite and enable us to subject her work to 'perverse' analysis. Such openness to the process of 'queering' makes her fictions at once challenging and rewarding – not only, but perhaps especially for lesbian readers.

6 Fatal Attractions: Feminist Theory and the Lesbian Lure

> The horror film consistently places the monster in conflict with the family, the couple and the institutions of patriarchal capitalism . . . The most persistent threat to the institution of heterosexuality . . . comes from the female vampire who preys on other women. Once bitten, the victim is never shy. She happily joins her female seducer, lost to the real world for ever.
>
> Barbara Creed, *The Monstrous-Feminine*

My main purpose in previous chapters has been to explore some of the most prominent, if not significant, configurations in which lesbian sexuality tends to emerge – or, as the case may be, become submerged – in the imaginary realm of twentieth-century Western culture, and to trace its destabilizing operations in various modes of 'fictional' discourse, especially literature and film. I have tried to show that, whether figuring overtly or covertly in a given text, and regardless of the author/director's gender, race, class and/or nationality, the appearance of the lesbian in heterosexual, or, more precisely, in heteropatriarchal contexts is closely bound up with questions of knowledge and meaning. That this should be so, derives from the fact that lesbian sexuality, falling outside the terms of 'the social contract', inevitably provokes a specific (though usually undefined) anxiety with respect to the mainstays of Western culture, that is, the stable operation of the system of gendered heterosexuality, and of identity-practices generally.

In the present chapter I wish to shift my focus away from 'the house of fiction', to recall Henry James's memorable phrase, to centre on its implied Other, and pursue my inquiry into the function and significance of female same-sex desire in the context of the discursive field usually designated 'non-fiction' and, more particularly, address the place of lesbian sexuality in feminist cultural criticism and theory.[1] I will read the lesbian's capricious, inescapably paradoxical presence in this discursive realm – or system of thought – through several earlier explorations of this kind, variously performed (and to different effects) by feminist theorists speaking from both lesbian and non-lesbian positions. A brief foray into psychoanalytic theory will subsequently allow me to draw a few tentative and as yet provisional conclusions as to the lesbian's critical place in academic feminist discourse, past as well as present.

As my pirating of its title in framing this discussion suggests, Judith Roof's *The Lure of Knowledge* is one of the enabling intertexts that have helped bring into sharper focus my increasingly troubled, yet heretofore somewhat confused thoughts about the lesbian's whereabouts in feminist criticism in the course of the past fifteen years or so.[2] Published in 1991, Roof's explorations stop at the end of what was by then a decade drawing to its close. The relevance of her comments nonetheless extends well beyond into the years that were to follow.

Since the latter half of the 1980s, Roof asserts, 'mainstream' (that is, white, middle class, heterosexual) feminism has sought to implement the lessons of diversity taught by poststructuralist and deconstructive theories by trying to incorporate multiple differences into our critical practices. Such apparent willingness to incorporate 'minority' voices, she observes, initially amounted to no more than a token acknowledgement of radically different perspectives.[3] As her careful readings incontrovertibly show, the representation of female diversity in feminist critical anthologies published in and around 1985 ('bumper year for a crop of feminist collections edited by established scholars and published by prestigious presses') often resulted in a reduction of multiple differences to mere 'deviance' from the mainstream. Apparently feeling they had therewith adequately met their political responsibilities, the editors of these books all took up a number of supposedly representative essays by black and/or lesbian authors, positioning them as a separate category in the collection, and/or placing them at the end of the volume. The issues raised by such 'deviant' voices were, however, unexceptionally situated in the context of – and hence contained within – (white, heterosexual, academic feminist) methodological debates. Programmatically inserted into the feminist mainstream, potentially disruptive minority discourses were consistently cast in the role of mere 'auxiliaries', reduced to mere 'players' in white, straight feminist discursive/political scripts. While attesting to their consciousness of diversity, mainstream critics could thus simultaneously foreground their claim to academic power by appearing to 'correct feminist homogeneity'.[4]

From the fact that the voices of radical difference were emphatically marked off as Other and, at the same time, placed within a 'general' feminist paradigm, Roof infers that diverse 'minority' perspectives were granted a discursive space in a gesture of 'critical separatism', so that excessive differences were 'made the same ... kept separate but equal'.[5] In addition to such practices of 'critical separatism', she notes a growing tendency to reduce all deviant voices to the 'formula "black and lesbian"'.[6] Regarded as mere variations on a single theme, that is, sexual difference, distinct modes of socio-cultural Otherness were formulaically aligned, and therewith neutralized. As a result, the destabilizing implications of alternative theoretical paradigms articulated by a variety of disparate Others could continue to go unrecognized, nor did their contributions need to be accepted as 'theoretical in themselves rather than as augmentative diversity'.[7] Presented as no more than so many forms of cultural diversity, deviant perspectives were hence categorically divested of their theoretical implications.

In an attempt to account for both the insistent (token) acknowledgement of diversity and the reduction of differences (in class, ethnicity and race in terms other than black) to the 'combination "black and lesbian"', Roof posits that, as 'displaced cast regular[s]', the incorporated instances of black and lesbian perspectives may be seen to function as 'the excess that disrupts the disrupters' of male culture. The inclusion of such Other perspectives to 'prove the efficacy of one or another mainstream critical philosophy' could therefore be 'construed as a fear that black and lesbian might upset that philosophy'. While ostensibly indicative of a willingness to confront the challenges of a radical concept of multiple differentiation, feminism's increasing emphasis on cultural diversity had, by the mid-1980s, on the one hand resulted in a newly articulated awareness of the pitfalls of a 'totalitarian' – if this time feminist – vision and, on the other, in a seemingly generous 'conciliatory takeover' of various Othernesses, so as to prevent the feminist applecart from being upset.[8]

The initially largely nominal recognition of black perspectives in feminist criticism gradually led to a growing awareness of the profound influence of racial differences on both cultural and theoretical practices. In contrast, lesbian and ethnic voices (other than black) continued to be kept 'separate but equal'. Pursuing her itinerary through the latter half of the 1980s, Roof notes a striking shift in emphasis in anthologizing practices of this period, an attempt at repoliticizing feminist literary criticism with the emergence of a 'new combo, race and class', and a concurrent 'de-emphasizing of lesbian sexuality'.[9] Public debates on 'political correctness' (as much as the conservative backlash in response to the demands of various 'minority' groups within institutions of higher education) ensued in an apparent need on the part of feminists to side with the most visibly oppressed. Against the background of neo-colonialist foreign policies operative in Euro-America during the Thatcher/Reagan years, multiculturalism and ethnic diversity became the passwords of a feminist project that considered itself 'coalesced with the range of diverse perspectives in a solidarity' against oppressive white male theory.[10] Around the same time, the figure of the lesbian disappeared from the theoretical arena altogether. If the lesbian makes an appearance at all in feminist critical discourse of the late 1980s, it tends to be as a largely 'apolitical category', while the effects of sexual orientation on critical theory and practice are only occasionally addressed; that is to say, only in relation to specific lesbian or bisexual writers. With the gradual dropping from sight of lesbian sexuality, the question of sexuality as such – as an epistemological and hence, political category – equally faded into the background. While the repoliticization of late 1980s feminist debates thus took the shape of an explicit solidarity with the most obviously underprivileged social groups, lesbian perspectives were essentially deprived of both their political and theoretical significance.

The depoliticization of lesbian sexuality within feminist critical discourse extends into the 1990s, and has not remained restricted to the 'politically correct' North American academy. This may, for instance, be gathered from a British anthology which, judging by its title, purported to constitute a move beyond the 1980s strategy of benevolent incorporation and/or assimilation with regard to radically Other perspectives. In their Preface to the volume in question, a collection of commissioned essays entitled *Destabilizing Theory: Contemporary Feminist Debates*, editors Michèle Barrett and Anne Phillips embrace the joint challenges offered by a 'politics of difference' to what they call the political project of ' "1970s western feminism" ', and the 'theoretical undermining of many of its paradigmatic assumptions'.[11] As a first motivating force behind such challenges, they identify 'current work of feminists on post-structuralist and post-modernist themes'. To this cryptic description of what was, in point of fact, no less than a major paradigm shift, they parenthetically add '(the charge that the specificity of black women's experience and the racism of white feminists had been ignored)'. Any indication as to the implications of this afterthought, or even a specification of who is doing the charging here, and who stands accused, is apparently considered unnecessary. Nor do the editors see fit to define their own positions in relation to either the charge or the implied acts of wilful ignorance. Conceding that their 'book does not aspire to be a total account of "feminism" ', being 'far from global in its reference points', they nonetheless claim to have addressed, from perspectives ranging 'beyond narrowly national or regional boundaries', the 'typical concerns of a western, academic feminist impulse ... that has come to see "western feminism" as an unstable and limited category'. The virtual slippage of ethnic or racial differences in this claim to diversity is in itself quite disturbing; what strikes me as even more remarkable, however, is that any awareness of sexual diversity and the potentially destabilizing effects of a specifically lesbian theoretical perspective are left out of this preamble (to what presents itself as a project of 'instability') altogether. To be fair, the question of lesbian sexuality is, in fact, addressed by one (token) essay included in the collection. Even so, the editors' lengthy Introduction which follows the Preface shows that the lesbian's 'curious habit of disappearing' (noted by Roof in feminist anthologies of the late 1980s), has by no means subsided in the present decade.[12]

For what are the 'key elements' informing the break-up of an earlier feminist 'consensus', according to Barrett and Phillips? In their introductory sketch of a now-diversified feminist project, they single out as a first differentiating element 'black women's critique of racist and ethnocentric assumptions of white feminists'. They go on to posit that the fragmentation characterizing the project of Western feminism since the 1980s has resulted in a renewed questioning of the notions of sexual difference and identity. In briefly discussing the backgrounds to these developments, they draw particular attention to a decided feminist 'unease' with regard to what were once 'confident distinctions between sex and gender', and a concurrent 'interest in psychoanalytic analyses of sexual difference and identity'. At this point, one would expect to find at least some acknowledgement of the pathbreaking theoretical work done in this field by radical lesbian thinkers, such as Judith Butler, Judith Roof and Teresa de Lauretis. However, in this retrospective outline of contemporary feminist theory, the concept of lesbian sexuality does not, in fact, make an appearance at all. What, in the view of Barrett and Phillips, the recent 'problematization' of sexual difference and identity has amounted to, is an 'analysis of women's experience of mothering', and, 'in its most "essentialist" moments, the celebration of Woman and her Womanly role'. Not only is the critical role of lesbian thinkers in 1980s feminist practice simply ignored, the notion of sexuality itself – lesbian or otherwise – is tacitly elided from the field of theory. Bracketed by, on the one hand, an emphasis on ethnic and racial differentiation and, on the other, the feminist engagement with 'post-structuralist and post-modernist ideas' (figuring as the third 'element' of disruption), the notion of 'sexual difference and identity', as it is presented here, does not allow for even a token appearance of the lesbian.[13] The potentially 'undermining' theoretical effects of sexual 'diversity' are thus conveniently glossed over. Couched within this tripartite mapping of the forces of disruption, lesbian sexuality is both rendered invisible and split off from the other two 'destabilizing' factors. Its covert positioning midways this narrative prelude at once signals the (repressed) centrality of lesbian sexuality in the history of feminist theory, and reinforces the prevalent notion of sexual deviance as an 'intermediate' stage in the development to theoretical maturity – even if an otherwise destabilized, for 'post-modernist', maturity.

Such a notable heterocentrist bias is equally apparent in feminist discourse outside the Anglograph critical community. In 1991–2, France saw the long-awaited publication of *Histoire des Femmes*, a five-volume history of gender in Europe from ancient Greece to today, edited by Georges Dubuy and Michelle Perrot.[14] The fruits of this monumental enterprise appeared in Dutch translation the following year, while the last remaining volume to be translated into English was published in 1994. In 1993, jointly reviewing the French original as well as the Dutch translation, lesbian historian Dorelies Kraakman presented the results of a careful perusal of all the variously indexed subjects that could possibly be related to lesbian sexuality. Having spent many hours eagerly scanning a total of ten hefty tomes, she found herself confronted, however, with a pervasive, indeed 'aggressive' silence on anything that might even suggest the (historical) existence of the 'love that dare not speak its name'. The 'equal indifference' towards lesbian love, sex and desire permeating this comprehensive overview of Women's History can only lead to the quite staggering conclusion that such a prestigious project of feminist scholarship has, in effect, no significance whatsoever for lesbian history. Or, as the disappointed reviewer herself tersely put it: 'Five Times Nothing Equals Nothing'.[15]

The instances of feminist discourse that I have (somewhat, but not quite, arbitrarily) singled out for my lesbian critique, seem to suggest that one can only deal with so much Otherness at once. While it would not just require another chapter but rather another book to explore the complex relations between differences in terms of sexuality and variegated ethnic and/or racial forms of Otherness, let alone critically to assess their respective and/or interactive operations within the general critical arena, the evidence suggests that, so far, the latter modes of differentiation have clearly won out on the former as far as theoretical prominence and thus academic visibility are concerned. I would, however, be willing to go a step further and suggest that the current emphasis on multiculturalism and ethnic diversity within feminist theory almost unexceptionally leads to a marked lack of attention to, if not suppression of, sexuality as an axis of exclusion, and, by extension, as a structural aspect of diverse forms of signifying processes, including theoretical practice. The consistent disappearance of the figure of the lesbian in feminist discourse cannot, it appears to me, be explained away as a twist of fate, or even as the result of historical accident – fortunate or unfortunate as the case may be. As a site of discursive absence, such non-figurations of lesbian sexuality should, as I have been arguing before, be read 'symptomatically' as precisely the kind of overdetermined ideological effect described by Frye as 'a scurrying to erase, to divert the eye, the attention, the mind'.[16]

Originally introduced, it seems by Gayatri Spivak,[17] Jane Gallop explains the practice of 'symptomatic reading' by setting it off against 'new critical close reading'. The latter mode of analysis, she suggests, 'embraces the text in order to more fully and deeply understand its excellences', while the former, coming out of 'psychoanalytic method by way of deconstruction', rather 'squeezes the text tight to force it to reveal its perversities'. Demystifying and hence diminishing the power of authoritative texts, a 'symptomatic' reading practice can at once be 'respectful, because closely attentive, and aggressive, because it wrests secrets the author might prefer to keep'.[18] What, then, could be the 'perversities' at once signalled and contained by the lesbian symptom – or rather, the symptom of its absence – so prominently present in the text of the majority of feminist discourse?[19] What could be the secrets that the highly diverse group of critics and theorists who, in some way or other, implicitly or explicitly claim 'authority' to speak (to) the feminist mainstream, would 'prefer to keep secret'?

To take these questions a little further, I will adopt Gallop's own backward glance at the coming-of-age of academic feminist literary theory, her controversial book *Around 1981*, as the second of my intertexts. I wish in particular to take up a few suggestions offered in a chapter whose title is (also) obliquely echoed in my own, 'The Attractions of Matrimonial Metaphor'.[20] Following a strategy similar to Roof's, Gallop performs detailed 'sympto-matic' readings of a number of 1980s critical anthologies in order to interrogate the decided heterotextual preference that informs both feminist editorial choices and the ways in which feminists have on the whole sought to (re)write the histories of their theo-retical and critical practices.[21] Gallop's major concern, as her chapter's title suggests, is with the questions how and why, in all of the texts subjected to her meticulous critical scrutiny, 'marriage functions as an allegory for feminist criticism.' She further seeks to link up the growing preoccupation with 'difference' – or, as the editors of one of the interrogated anthologies insist, with 'making a difference' – with the persistent 'choice of marriage as central metaphor' in academic feminist writings. Whilst running her diag-nostic tests, Gallop, not surprisingly, repeatedly refers to lesbian critics and theorists so as to expose more effectively the hetero-sexist trends qualifying the work of their mainstream 'sisters'. And while it is never explicitly stated in precisely these terms, her foregrounding of lesbianism throughout, but especially in the concluding section of her argument, suggests that by 'making a place' for such a deviant sex/textual preference, feminist criticism and theory might really succeed in 'making a difference'.[22]

Before she reaches this conclusion, Gallop has sought to eluci-date the 'attraction of matrimonial metaphor' by pointing to fem-inism's implicated position in the structures of (heterosexual) gender ideology. She submits that the 'internalized heterosexual-ity' of much feminist theory may be read as part of the 'hetero-sexual teleology' implicit in Western culture generally and in the practice of literary theory in particular. Rhetorically asking whether 'we prefer sexual difference because this particular dif-ference conventionally promises narrative solution', Gallop analyses the desire underlying 'heterosexist' feminist textual prac-tice as a fundamental desire for 'a happy ending' within a cultural plot of otherwise irreducible differences. The focus on gender can thus be seen to reinstate the promise of what Cora Kaplan has called the 'inevitable resolution' to the plot of heterosexuality, the dominant cultural scenario in relation to which other social/theoretical divisions and deviations operate as mere 'narra-tive backdrop or minor stumbling-block[s]'.[23]

Interestingly, Gallop's own text would appear to prove her

point quite convincingly: in the Afterword to *Around 1981*, which functions as a sort of retrospective impression of the years separating the completion of the manuscript (around 1991) from the period covered by it (up to around 1987), the figure of the lesbian 'inevitably' fades into the shadows of the narrative stage. The primary focus of Gallop's résumé is the successful contestation of the ethnocentrist bias of Euro-American feminism, first by African-American feminists, and increasingly also by women of other ethnic groups and nationalities. While this parting gesture redresses a relative neglect of issues like race and ethnicity in earlier chapters, it equally points up the very 'symptomaticity' of lesbian invisibility in feminist discourse that Gallop herself has taken such pains to expose and denounce. Significantly, 'gay studies' do briefly make an appearance, that is, in relation to a perceived shift in feminist theoretical attention from 'women' to 'gender'. Linked up with the new interest in 'men, masculinity, and even their own will to mastery' among feminists, 'gay studies' are, I think quite rightly, identified as a field of (potentially problematic) intersection and overlap with feminist criticism.[24] Be that as it may, near the point of narrative closure, even Gallop's rigorous practice of self-consciousness thus does not prevent her from falling prey to the attractions of matrimonial metaphor: as a symptom of her relapse into the addictive longing for a 'happy ending', we find, once again, (gay) men and (straight) women united, and a concurrent, silent elision of the figure of the lesbian.

My third major intertext, Teresa de Lauretis' powerful and thought-provoking study of lesbian sexuality, *The Practice of Love*, allows me both to continue and complicate the intertextual traces that frame this discussion. In a chapter entitled 'The Seductions of Lesbianism: Feminist Psychoanalytic Theory and the Maternal Imaginary', de Lauretis sets the stage for the 'model of "perverse" desire' that it is the purpose of her book to unfold and that reaches its culmination in the subsequent chapter. Against the background of psychoanalytic theory, she interrogates the function of lesbianism in feminist discourse through an investigation of yet another of feminism's favourite tropes, the 'maternal imaginary', or the metaphor of the mother.[25]

The psychoanalytic situation, de Lauretis points out, and

especially the process of transference, hinges on a 'logic of seduction' in which the (young female) patient performs a role as desirous agent in relation to the (older male) doctor.[26] Even though the analytic relationship as such was inevitably cast within the constraining patriarchal structures of his time, Freud's female patients – hysterics and other 'psychically deviants' – thus refuted what prevailing juridical, philosophical and scientific discourses and, indeed, Lacanian psychoanalysis, as well as much feminist theory today, consider a fundamental *im*possibility, that is, the conjunction of female agency and desire, of women having the 'power of seducing *and of being seduced*, being ... sexed and desiring subjects' [emphasis is de Lauretis'].[27] Having 'managed to envisage at least some women ... as sexed subjects and as subjects of desire', Freudian psychoanalysis must therefore be granted the honour of having created the 'possibility of female subject *and* desire'.[28]

Continuing on a line frankly characterized as a speculative one, de Lauretis subsequently posits that lesbianism 'performs, within feminist theory and vis-à-vis the question of female subjectivity and desire, a role analogous to that of psychoanalysis', in that the figure of the lesbian in contemporary feminist discourse represents the possibility of female desire without the consequent loss of subjectivity (that is, the 'normal' configuration of female subjectivity within the system of gendered heterosexuality). In other words, while by no means suggesting that all women are (closeted) lesbians, the analogy seeks to convey that lesbianism, or rather, 'female homosexuality', cannot but play a critical role in the feminist imaginary because, as a fantasmatic structure, an envisaged possibility, it – and it alone – can serve to guarantee 'women the status of sexed and desiring subjects, wherever their desire may be directed' in psychosocial reality.[29] Feminist psychoanalytic theory has hence been able to '[reclaim] homosexuality as a prerogative or a component of female sexuality', without, however, sufficiently taking into account the specificity of lesbian sexuality. Indeed, more often than not, such theories succeed in completely 'eliding [the latter's] psychic and social differences from heterosexuality'.[30]

The assimilation of lesbianism to a 'female homosexuality' that guarantees the female subject's desire is facilitated through and by the operations of a 'maternal imaginary' in feminist discourse, usually taking the shape of an idealized construction of a mother/daughter-bond projected as a founding 'homosexual' relation common to all women. Some branches of psychoanalytic feminist theory have sought to overcome the reign of the phallus, or the Paternal Law, by envisioning or (re)creating a maternal symbolic, reinstating the mother at the point of origin of female subjectivity, and therewith reinscribing the pre-Oedipal, or pre-symbolic origins of female identification. Others have expressly sought to reincorporate the erotic aspects of the primary bond between mother and child, so as to charge Oedipal female subjectivity with the empowering force of (same-sex) desire. De Lauretis rightly insists, however, that woman-identification and sexual object-choice cannot be regarded as the same, either on the intra-psychic or on socio-symbolic levels, nor even be considered to constitute a continuum–feminist appropriations of Rich's notion of a 'lesbian continuum' notwithstanding.[31] In her critical rereadings of various feminist rewritings of the 'maternal metaphor', she effectively shows that it is precisely in their respective relations to the mother – Oedipal or pre-Oedipal, phallic or feminist – that the differences between lesbian and female subjectivity obtain and, consequently, most strikingly reveal themselves. It would take me too far to trace the intricacies of the careful textual analyses that pave the way for the further development of de Lauretis' 'model of "perverse" desire'. What is most immediately relevant to my own argument here is that her explorations of the 'maternal imaginary' in feminist discourse accurately pinpoint the ambivalence of the figure of the lesbian within its conceptual realm.

If the projection of a founding 'female homosexuality' enables the conceptualization of woman as libidinal agent, of the female subject as a subject of desire, the actualization of such female same-sex desire, indeed, its socio-symbic personification in the shape of the lesbian, simultaneously threatens the dissolution of that very subjectivity. Within the terms of the founding social contract – indeed, within the conceptual framework underlying Western reality as a whole – 'woman' has, to recall Wittig's provocative assertions, 'meaning only in heterosexual systems of thought and heterosexual economic systems'.[32] In other words, feminists committed to the task of female resistance and empowerment, but who nonetheless, by loving and living with men, locate themselves in their 'normal' positions within the system of gendered heterosexuality, cannot but have fundamentally ambivalent stakes in the fantasmatic structure, the 'possibility of subject *and* desire', embodied by the figure of the lesbian. The implementation of the 'maternal-homosexual metaphor' in feminist discourse hence at once signals and serves to smooth over contradictions inherent in the critical project of feminism itself.

Blurring the distinction between feminism and lesbianism – or rather, assimilating the latter to the former (as, for instance, exemplified by the consistent metaphorization of the 'lesbian *existence*' that forms the core of Rich's critical vision on compulsory heterosexuality), the variegated inscriptions of the maternal image in feminist texts together make up a 'composite figure of symbolic mother' that, de Lauretis infers, indisputably 'gestures toward lesbianism'. But insofar as feminism refuses to 'dig up and confront its deeply ambivalent stakes' in lesbianism,[33] its troping on the 'maternal-homosexual' factor can never be more than that, and feminist theories of desire may never move beyond the inefficacy of equivocal gesturing. The lesbophobic undercurrents that, though shifting in strength and to different effects, have informed feminism from the early days of the Women's Liberation Movement onwards, can hence continue to go largely unchallenged.

In earlier chapters, I have argued that dominant or 'malestream' culture seeks to suppress the threat of lesbian Otherness by turning it into a titillating spectacle to be subsumed by, if not violently obliterated within, the myth of masculinity. Mainstream feminism has, in the course of the past decades, and with considerable success, managed to wipe lesbianism off the political and theoretical agenda by implementing similarly effective methods of discursive containment, variously having recourse to the strategies of subordination, tokenism, assimilation and/or muting. The net results, however, are not as dissimilar as the respective socio-cultural locations of these diametrically opposed discourses would lead us to expect. The lesbian spectre – never more than a shadowy, derivative figure within the system of gendered heterosexuality subtending both modes of discourse – haunts the edges of either field of power/knowledge as a minor irregularity or, more accurately, constitutes a negative presence within them. But if the effects of masculist versus feminist lesbophobia are not entirely irreconcilable, both the underlying stakes and the methods or mechanisms that bring about the alarming subject's overall 'negativization' differ significantly from one discourse to the other.

De Lauretis' main supporting metaphor, 'the seductions of lesbianism', aptly points up that, within the context of feminist discourse, the fantasmatic structure of female same-sex desire exerts the power of attraction; an attraction, however, not just to the thing itself, but one that threatens to deflect, distract or side-track from a proper course.[34] In our postmodern, and, as some would prefer to believe, 'postfeminist' times, the idea of woman's 'proper place' clearly no longer holds sway as it has throughout the almost twenty centuries of Western history. Feminism has undeniably been one of the central forces behind the demystification of precisely those organizing myths that would confine women to their proper place in heteropatriarchy. Indeed, virtually flying in the face of the Laws of Nature, it has succeeded in luring many a woman away from what even Freud considered their biological destiny.[35] But despite feminism's manifest success at disrupting male culture on a social level, the enduring 'attraction of matrimonial metaphor' and the seductive powers of the 'homosexual-maternal metaphor' that speak (through) its critical and theoretical discourses signify that two of the mainstays of dominant culture – the intertwining myths of marriage and motherhood – have hardly lost their spellbinding force on an imaginary, even symbolic level. Nor, it should be clear by now, has feminism done much – if anything – to dislodge the lesbian from her accustomed place as the site of the abject in the collective imagination. The myth of the devouring lesbian is still going strong; translated into the popular image of the monstrous seducer that would lead woman astray, beguile her into forsaking her proper role within the Oedipal drama of institutionalized heterosexuality, the fatal attractions of this figure speak equally through dominant cultural texts as they transpire in feminist discursive practices.

Taken together, the enduring strength of these myths, and

especially their powerful, albeit largely unacknowledged, operation within feminist discourse, adequately attest to the latter's stakes in what Gallop calls the 'heterosexual teleology' underlying Western culture generally and the practice of literary criticism in particular. But this, as de Lauretis persuasively argues, is not the whole story, for it is precisely its fearful fascination with the figure of the lesbian – whether disguised in the metaphor of the 'female homosexual', the 'maternal-homosexual' or the 'symbolic mother' – which underscores the fundamental ambivalence that lies at the heart of the feminist project *per se*. To explain what I mean by this, I must make a brief detour into psychoanalytic theory, and in particular focus on those psychic processes that Freud has put into circulation under the heading of 'defence mechanisms'.

Embodying both a promise (of female agency and desire) and a threat (the dissolution of the distinction between the sexes), the mythical figure of the lesbian calls forth a number of discrete yet interrelated methods of discursive containment that find their respective correlates in various aspects of the defensive process in the psychoanalytic sense. The term 'defence' (*Abwehr*) in Freud denotes a variety of psychic operations that each in their own way seek to reduce or eliminate anything that poses a threat to the integrity and stability of the ego. The ego is that part of the personality responsible for staving off internal conflicts and contradictions, and that furthermore produces 'unpleasurable affect' when the concrete content of an act of thought (an 'idea' or 'representation') appears incompatible with itself. As both the product of bio-psychological stabilization and responsible for its maintenance, the ego is, Laplanche and Pontalis affirm, 'both the *stake* and the *agent* of [defensive] operations'.[36]

The defensive process is a normal part of psychic reality, insofar as it protects the individual from the destabilizing effects of distressing experiences. After an initial experience of unpleasure, the ego sets up 'protective shields' that serve to filter and deflect the intensity of unpleasure in case such an experience is revived in later life. In his theory of defence, Freud maintains a distinction between 'external excitations on the one hand, from which flight is possible or against which a damming mechanism is set up

... and, on the other hand, *internal* excitations which it is impossible to evade'. It is the latter kind of threat to the ego, that is, 'aggression from the inside', that may lead to various modalities of 'pathological defence'.[37] One of the most familiar (if misunderstood) instances of psychic defence is 'repression' (*Verdrängung*).[38] In the process of repression, the subject tries to relegate to the unconscious those representations (thoughts, memories, images) that, being bound to an instinct, risk provoking unpleasure. If successful, the instinctual affect and the idea (or representation) are jointly split off from the subject's conscious and become virtually 'unknowable' to it. This splitting process is not in itself pathological; it is, in effect, the way the unconscious comes into being at all. In its pathological mode (as, for instance, in hysteria or obsessional neurosis), the effects of such a relegation of conscious materials to the unconscious, however, become manifest in the form of symptoms – the 'return of the repressed' – that, traced to their rightful origins in analysis, allow the patient to recover parts of their 'forgotten' experience, to remember what had been split off and thus lost from consciousness. Once recalled, such previously completely inaccessible, indeed 'non-existent', experiences are perfectly vivid memories in the subject's conscious thought.

In the psychic process of defence the representation or idea of unpleasure does not stay fixed (as is the case in repression), but becomes separated from the affect to which it was originally bound. Split off from each other, the instinctual affect and the memory, image, fantasy or thought to which it was attached are subsequently subject to different procedures. One of the most common modes of defence is the mechanism of 'disavowal' (*Verleugnung*), a term Freud primarily invokes in connection with castration. Upon perceiving the woman's 'lack' of a penis, children of either sex initially refuse to acknowledge this fact, and maintain their belief in its presence until the Oedipus complex, with its threat of paternal castration, forces them to abandon this (mis)perception. Unlike repression, which is first and foremost an internal affair, involving a conflict between ego and instinct, disavowal additionally affects external reality. It entails a refusal of a recognized perception, a simultaneous acknowledgement and disavowal of a perceived reality, in particular that of the woman's lack. If, Freud elucidates, 'we wish to differentiate between what happens to the *idea* as distinct from the *affect*, we can restrict "repression" to relate to the affect; the correct word for what happens to the idea is then "denial" '.[39] Maintaining two incompatible positions at once, the ego itself consequently undergoes a process of splitting: one part recognizes the reality of the traumatic perception, while another persists in refusing to do so.

Laplanche and Pontalis note that, from 1927 onwards, Freud's elaboration of the notion of disavowal 'relates essentially to the special case of fetishism'.[40] A fetish is anything that enables the subject to deny the reality of an unwelcome perception, most especially that of the absent female penis, by providing a substitute for that which is perceived lacking. In the normal case, the little boy at some point in the Oedipal process is forced both to acknowledge sexual difference and to give up his belief in the maternal phallus, compelled by the threat of castration represented by paternal prohibition, the 'real' phallus. The boy who persists in disavowing the woman's 'castration' in the face of the paternal threat – that is, the possibility of losing his own highly-prized organ – constructs in his psychic reality another part of the female body, or any other object in external reality, that may serve as a 'penis-substitute'. This substitute or fetish subsequently comes to function as a 'token of triumph over the threat of castration and a safeguard against it', and, in its designated role as 'female phallus', furthermore constitutes a source of sexual pleasure. One of its advantages for the subject is, Freud almost enviously remarks, that the significance of fetishes is 'not known to the world at large and therefore not prohibited; they are easily available and sexual gratification by their means is thus very convenient.' Accordingly, few of his patients who also turned out to be fetishists considered themselves in any way ill on that account; on the contrary, Freud observes, they 'are usually quite content with [their fetishes] or even extol the advantages they offer for erotic gratification'.[41] That the founder of psychoanalysis, despite his recognition of such 'contentment', nonetheless numbers fetishism among the 'sexual perversions' derives from the fundamental ambivalence, the splitting of the ego, that forms the core of phenomenon.

In the psychic process that underlies the fetishist's perversion, the separation of affect from its representation, the perception of lack persists, but 'a very energetic action has been exerted to keep up the denial of it.'[42] Where the construction of the substitute-object or fetish itself requires a substantial amount of psychic investment, its 'upkeep' in adult life continues to make considerable demands on the subject's energies, for the substitute-object additionally forms a 'sort of permanent memorial' of the 'horror of castration' that has issued in its creation. Apart from exerting continuous defensive action (generally only showing up in the guise of symptoms under analytic scrutiny), the fetishist harbours a permanent 'aversion from the female genitals' which 'remains as an indelible stigma of the repression'.[43] While to some extent both advantageous and gratifying, the psychic split that forms the foundation of the fetishist's (phallic) security renders the phenomenon as a whole ultimately ambivalent to the point of pathology. Involving the coexistence of two different forms of ego-defence, one of these protective measures (the disavowal of a perception) is directed towards external reality. The fetishist's compulsive protection of the heavily invested substitute-object hence entails a denial, however partial, of external reality, which is always in danger of slipping into the more substantial denial, or complete loss of reality, that characterizes psychosis.

I have gone into these issues at some length because the processes of disavowal, and particularly, its 'special case', fetishism, shed significant light on the mottled career of the lesbian in feminist theory. It hardly needs pointing out that Freud did not consider fetishism, out of all the perversions, to be applicable to women: always already dispossessed, they have nothing to lose and would thus have no need to create a substitute-penis to guarantee their own 'treasured organ' to begin with. What is more, the implied centrality of the threat of castration and, more specifically, the threatening force behind it, underscores, de Lauretis astutely remarks, the 'fundamental role in fetishism of the *paternal* phallus', as opposed to the (merely ostensibly pivotal) maternal one.[44] Despite Freud's insistence on the specific nature of that which supposedly calls forth the fetish, the 'particular quite special penis' the boy 'once believed in and does not wish to forego', that is, the 'woman's (mother's) phallus', it is the father's prohibition, the actual threat of the subject's own castration which sets the perverse defence process properly in motion.

Freud's persistent phallocentric leanings have not prevented lesbian psychoanalytic theorists, especially in more recent years, from appropriating the notion of fetishism so as to make both it – to various intents and purposes – and the concomitant possibility of creating a substitute-phallus, available to lesbian subjects as well.[45] However, since my main concern in this chapter is not psychoanalytic theory, nor even (lesbian) sexuality *per se*, I wish to pursue my inquiry into the function of the figure of the lesbian in feminist theory by shifting my focus from the intra-psychic realm to that of language, in order to make the fetishist perversion equally available to the feminist subject. To this end, I will proceed by attempting to forge a link between the Freudian notion of fetishism, particularly in its connection with castration, and the Lacanian rereading of psychoanalysis from the perspective of modern linguistics. It is, after all, primarily in the realm of language, or discourse, that feminism's 'deeply ambivalent stakes' in lesbianism, *qualitate qua*, most forcefully obtain.

Within the context of Lacanian thought, the Freudian notion of castration is displaced onto language to become the paradigm of what is rearticulated as 'symbolic castration'. With this term, Lacan first of all refers to the loss of the Real, that is, the breakup of the primordial mother/child-dyad upon the infant's perception of its own reflection in the mirror. A culminating moment in the earliest stage of subjective formation, the end of the 'mirror stage' constitutes the trauma of primary alienation: what the child henceforth will come to accept as her/his self, is no more than an illusion of identity, an imaginary construction of Self in/by that which is utterly Other.[46] The second critical moment in the process of subjectivity occurs somewhat later, when the child enters into language, and therewith learns to identify her/himself by means of the symbolic markers that organize the social order. Assuming her/his appropriate place in the discursive realm, that is, the pre-existing field of power/knowledge in which each individual must assume a position in order to become a full subject, s/he acquires, among other things, a recognizable gender identity. At once marking the onset of the subjective process and the traumatic rupture that puts an end to pre-symbolic bliss, the primary moment of symbolic castration does not yet recognize sexual difference: male and female subjects are equally symbolically castrated.[47] (The fact that women nonetheless principally carry the social and political weight of this primary loss has more to do with established power relations than with psychosexual realities.)

Lacan's rereading of Freud thus renders the notion of castration itself into a variously significant process in which language plays a key, if not determining, role. Yet here too, the two interrelated defence mechanisms of disavowal and fetishism play crucial, indeed, quite similar parts. In Lacan's recast Oedipal scenario, Freudian castration anxiety translates into a process in which the male subject perceives but refuses to acknowledge his castrated condition – he imagines himself to be in possession of the phallus – and displaces his fear of losing the vital instrument onto the female subject, or rather, onto her body. The female body's physical 'lack' becomes the symbol of what he has to lose and is therewith transformed into a fantasmatic fetish/phallus. Woman, in Lacan, does not in fact exist, except as the absolute Other in phallocentric representation. Embodying (quite literally) that which must be continually conquered and appropriated to authenticate the male's non-castrated existence, female 'lack' serves to guarantee the man's continued possession of the phallus, of what Lacan calls the 'ultimate signifier'. In such a framework, the difference between male and female subjectivity is thus a question of either having or being the phallus/ultimate signifier.

However, if we pursue the Lacanian idea of castration a little further, and assume that male and female subjects are equally symbolically castrated, what can we observe about the operations of such protective mechanisms as disavowal and fetishization in relation to the female psyche? Who or what can be set up as the fetish/phallus that must simultaneously symbolize and mask her inescapably castrated condition? Or, to return to the question which initiated this enquiry: who or what might serve as a screen onto which the feminist theoretical subject can project her lack of symbolic power, of discursive authority within the social order – a lack which she, in claiming subjective agency *and* desire, cannot but refuse to accept? In view of the evidence generated by my earlier interactions with various feminist intertexts, it would not seem too far-fetched to suggest that it is the figure of the lesbian and, more specifically, the lesbian theoretical subject who enjoys the dubious pleasure of being persistently cast in the privileged role of feminist fetish/phallus.

One might at this point object, however, that the transpositional manoeuvre such a proposition entails is theoretically untenable and, at best, politically unwarranted. For how, one might well ask, can the Freudian concept of disavowal, conceived as a protective strategy on the part of the individual (male) psyche, via Lacan, be read back into the predominantly public realm of feminist theoretical practice? And what good would it do the feminist cause to perform such a hazardous move? In order to account for my proposition's underlying motives, I must momentarily backtrack on the foregoing argument.

In Freudian terms, as we have seen, the strategy of disavowal revolves around a very specific psychic operation: the splitting of the ego, in which an affect becomes disconnected from its representation so as to allow for either part to be subjected to different defensive procedures (or *vice versa*, for the process is, in effect, mutually constitutive).[48] The disavowed object which is the result of this procedure represents the repressed contents of a simultaneously acknowledged and repudiated (for unwanted) psychic perception, yet, at one or more removes: the unwelcome (part of) reality has been turned into something else, has found its substitute or, as Freud puts it, 'has been appointed its successor'.[49]

As a fantasmatic structure, lesbian sexuality, or so de Lauretis contends, guarantees not only the possibility of female same-sex desire, but of female desire *tout court*. At the same time, the seductive figure of the lesbian poses a threat to female agency, in that it throws into confusion, indeed, thoroughly calls into question the system of compulsive heterosexuality on which the dual categories of gender, male and female, necessarily depend. Moreover, by claiming the status of subjective agents for women within the binary terms of the heterosexual gender system, feminist discourse remains, we have seen Gallop argue, deeply if not inextricably embedded in the very structures of power/knowledge that insist on the 'impossibility of [female] subject *and* desire'. The symbolic value of lesbianism, or 'female homosexuality', as an empowering fantasmatic structure hence cannot but be of a highly mixed, if not contradictory nature; as contradictory, in fact, as the value of any substitute-object that owes its construction to a fundamental split in the subject's consciousness. While explaining the profoundly ambivalent stakes of feminism in lesbianism – as much as its reluctance to 'dig up and confront' them – the psychoanalytic gloss on the splitting of the ego in the process of disavowal may therefore equally help further to elucidate the unhappy fate of the lesbian, and of lesbian theory, in feminist discourse.

In the normative terms of heteropatriarchal thought, only those who are – or, more accurately, who consider themselves to be – in possession of the phallus can be subjects of desire. Woman, in her designated role as substitute for the 'ultimate signifier', must give up her claim to the phallus in order to attain adult subjecthood. De Lauretis' speculations about lesbianism as a fantasmatic structure, as the envisaged possibility (or psychic perception) of 'female subject *and* desire', suggest that the embodiment of such a possibility would represent precisely the kind of fatal attraction to feminist consciousness as would call forth the defensive splitting of the ego that forms the essence of fetishism. If the analogy I am tentatively implying here holds true – and *pace* Roof, I am doing so fully aware that 'all analogies are faulty' – we could hence, in our turn, speculate that the perceived reality of lesbianism creates a conflict in the subject of feminism which requires the putting into operation of the two forms of defence that jointly constitute the process of disavowal operative in fetishism, that is, repression and denial. Let me try to trace the implications of this in somewhat more detail.

The affective value of the perception of female same-sex desire is, in feminist discourse, subjected to the defensive mechanism of repression, split off from consciousness, and relegated to the realm of the unconscious, the dark continent reigned over by the pre-Oedipal mother. Its disconnected representation, the figure of the lesbian, in contrast, undergoes a series of transformations in a process which precludes its secret significance 'on the inside' from being revealed to the world 'outside'. Elusive metaphors consequently variously stand in for, or are appointed the 'successors' of the disavowed (lesbian) object, such as, 'female homosexuality', the 'homosexual-maternal', the 'symbolic mother', or even such an ostensibly unlikely figure as 'heterosexual marriage', as it surfaces in feminism's perpetual pursuit of teleological closure, its obsessive quest for 'inevitable' narrative resolutions.

As the guarantee of female desire, the fantasmatic structure of lesbianism, as well as the ever more elusive metaphoric guises under which it materializes in feminist discourse, can thus be argued to perform a role as substitute-object, a fetish, which simultaneously functions as a 'token of triumph over the threat of castration', the loss of symbolic agency, and as a safeguard against such a loss. Freud reminds us, however, that 'the horror of castration', precisely by creating its substitute-object, at the same time sets up a 'permanent memorial of itself'. These profoundly contradictory effects of the fetishist impulse would appear adequately to explain the practice of tokenism characterizing feminist literary critics' editorial attitudes toward lesbianism during the early 1980s, and furthermore shed significant light on its co-runner and successor, the compulsive 'gesturing' towards lesbianism in feminist psychoanalytic theory in more recent years. Still, even if the suggested analogy allows us, to some extent, to untangle the marked duplicity in feminist dealings with lesbianism, it does not, at least not in any satisfactory manner, account for the equally frequently encountered gesture by which the subject of lesbianism tends 'curiously' to disappear behind the feminist political horizon, or is simply eclipsed from its critical and theoretical discourse altogether. I will come back to this in a moment.

Freud's paper on fetishism contains one further observation that renders his ideas on its 'perverse' practices particularly relevant to the questions at hand. There is one symptom, he reassuringly remarks, that is 'never lacking in any fetishist', and that is an 'aversion from the real female genitals', the terrifying perception of which has enforced the setting up of the substitute-object in the first place. The residue of that first horror, the symptomatic *abhorrence* invoked by the psychic perception of lack, thus 'remains as an indelible stigma of the repression'.[50] In the context of the analogy I am proposing, such symptomatic aversion would appear to find an adequate correlate in feminism's largely unacknowledged, yet structurally underlying, internalized lesbophobia. Nonetheless, since the process of disavowal operative in fetishism critically hinges on an ambivalence which necessitates a splitting between affect and idea, between instinct and representation, feminism's fetishization of lesbian sexuality does not merely produce (arguably harmful) effects on an internal level. Indeed, as we have seen, the difference between repression *per se* and the more elaborate defensive procedure of fetishization, is that the latter's effects do *not* remain restricted to the internal realm of psychic reality only: its distinguishing trait is precisely that, while comprising a self-protective response to 'aggression from the inside', it also critically affects the world of external reality. To the extent, then, that feminism (as yet) shows little willingness to interrogate its 'deeply ambivalent' stakes in lesbianism, it will continue to play into the hands of, if not reinforce its complicity with, an external larger culture in which the lesbian cannot but be a site of negativity and/or absence. In other words, insofar as the feminist engagement with lesbianism fails to move beyond the reinscription of attractions offered by the alluring metaphors haunting its interior, it will reinforce rather than contest regimes of power/knowledge in which the lesbian spectre, to recall Butler's evocative phrases, can never be more than a 'derivative example, a shadow of the real', an impossible figure that must continually be relegated to the realm of the abject, to the 'unspeakable', abhorrent and abhorred underside of external heteropatriarchal reality.[51]

Now, briefly to come back to the question put aside a moment ago, the presumed interconnections between lesbianism, the abject and the cultural unconscious would also begin to explain the gradual disappearance of lesbian sexuality in a process of elimination that, finding its starting-point in feminist discourse of the late 1980s, continues to this very day. For if the all but complete eclipse of the figure of the lesbian cannot be interpreted in terms of either repression or disavowal, it does invoke yet another of the Freudian defence mechanisms, one that is, in effect, even more directly generated by anxiety, that is, the strategy of 'negation' (*Verneinung*). In its psychoanalytic sense, the process of negation entails that the 'ideational content of what is repressed' is temporarily prevented from reaching consciousness. Its outcome is a 'kind of intellectual acceptance of the repressed, while at the same time what is essential to the repression persists'.[52] In order to achieve the required effects, negation implies that unwanted psychic materials, prior to being repressed, are both verbally and emotionally articulated, albeit in negative terms. It follows that the unconscious contents of the repressed are at once denied and confirmed, for in order to be liable to negation they must have been posited first.

The intertwining operations of these variously combined yet distinct defensive strategies suggest that the figure of the lesbian has, over the past fifteen years, served as a shield to protect feminism against the risks of losing its voice in a complex and shifting manner. Transformed into an apolitical, non-epistemological category, the radical difference of lesbian desire is first of all prevented from endangering the stability of female subjecthood and discursive agency. As a disavowed object moreover, the subject of these 'perverse' desires proves eminently suited to play its role as fetish, as feminism's 'token of triumph' over the threat of symbolic castration, as well as constituting a 'permanent memorial' of the scene of such horror. As a site of negativity, the lesbian figure is additionally capable of at once symbolizing and masking such dangers as follow from a genuine attempt at recognizing the possible blind spots of longstanding, often ardently cherished conceptual paradigms, especially those founded on an exclusionary and oppositional notion of heterosexual difference.

Seen in this light, it is not so surprising that the lesbian spectre, after a few token appearances on the discursive stage, was compelled to move back into the feminist closet precisely around the time when media throughout the Western world began to celebrate the beginning of a new 'postfeminist' era. In the mid-1980s what little social authority feminism had, with great difficulty, acquired came newly under threat from what was soon to become a full-blown 'anti-feminist backlash', a threat which has hardly diminished since.[53] With the almost simultaneous emergence of a multicultural *Zeitgeist*, the lesbian abject/object could apparently still function as a screen onto which feminists could project their (undoubtedly justified) fear of a further loss of symbolic authority. Fear, however, has never been a reliable counsellor. Within an increasingly differentiated, if not diffracting socio-cultural realm, in which all sorts of phobias seem to become, and with alarming ease at that, an acceptable part of the even most liberal of official discourses, any critical project committed to a radical political agenda would do well not to heed such counsel.

Let me therefore, in conclusion, return to and complete, Henry James's phrase partly quoted at the beginning of this chapter: 'The house of fiction has many windows.' The same holds true for the 'house of theory', and particularly that of feminist theory. Rather than continuing to be lured by the fatal attractions of elusive metaphors, feminism should, at this point in time, be ready to give up its reluctance to 'dig up and confront' its stakes in lesbianism. The tantalizing subject, it seems to me, demands as much as it deserves a full political and theoretical hearing.

Epilogue

When a subject is highly controversial – and any question about sex is that – one cannot hope to tell the truth. One can only show how one came to hold whatever opinion one does hold. One can only give one's audience the chance of drawing their own conclusions as they observe the limitations, the prejudices, the idiosyncrasies of the speaker.

Virginia Woolf, *A Room of One's Own*

Nearing the end of my exploratory journey through various sections of the Eurowestern cultural realm, having traced its fault lines to learn more about, peek at, or even 'find' the elusive figure of the lesbian somehow somewhere hovering in its variously defined off-spaces, 'knowing' she is there and knowing that I want to find 'her', I find myself resisting. I find myself resisting the moment of closure that is also that of unclosure, that long-awaited moment at which a triumphant, revelatory gesture succeeds in finally resolving the riddle that forms both the heart and the starting-point of the traditional quest narrative – scholarly or otherwise. Intent upon bringing this project to its prerequisite and, indeed, inevitable ending – however provisional or temporary this may be – I hesitate to embrace the challenge of the unravelling revelation. Something stands in the way of my desire to reach the liberating, concluding moment that would untie the knot of the myriad discursive threads it has been the purpose of this book to pursue, analyse and criticize and that, paradoxically, simultaneously would enable me to tie them up differently, to make them *mean* differently, to realize the 'envisaged possibility' at the end of the rainbow in my conceptual universe. Whence this resistance and reluctance? Why not offer my readers (and myself) an ingenious, composite answer, in which would be combined all the partial solutions that I have, sometimes confidently, sometimes more cautiously, but at least with a distinct degree of self-assurance been willing or eager to propose in the foregoing chapters? Is it because, in a discursive quest aimed at locating the 'impossible' cultural figure of the lesbian, such a moment of closure, the 'inevitable resolution' of conventional narrative plots is simply not available? Or is it because I do not really want to know, do not really wish to discover or, better still, *un*cover the 'truth' about the lesbian subject in the Western cultural imagination that I keep postponing that moment? Is it, in other words, the sway of the phallus, which, Lacan tells us, can play its role only when veiled, that prevents me from entering the stage of discursive finalization, in that such a discovery would put a definitive end to my quest? As is the case with most etiological questions, the answer here would, I suspect, lie somewhere in the middle – which is the same as saying that there simply is no clear-cut answer. And it is perhaps this very unanswerability, this inconclusiveness, as its finds expression in a thwarting resistance to closure, that will yet allow me to take this inquiry to what can only be a partial, provisional and transitory ending.

Resistance, as Freud discovered, and as Shoshana Felman helpfully reminds us, is a 'textual knot, a nodal point of unknown significance, the navel of an unknown text'.[1] As a speaking subject, as a subject of knowledge *and* desire, my consciousness of my self as a being-in-the-world can never fully coincide with the practice of my thought. Insofar as thought exceeds consciousness, that is to say, insofar as the process of knowing extends into the 'unknown', or unknowable, my resistance to closure may turn out to have a significance that cannot yet be seen by me, that may only be discerned by (future) readers of this book.

By thus foregrounding the autobiographical groundings of my critical practice, I am not suggesting that, being necessarily subjective, such readings as I have presented here are contingent to the extent of total arbitrariness. Acknowledging the bounded character of critical readings, that is, the reading/writing subject's situatedness in the perceived reality of her 'real' life, does not imply that, as far as questions of meaning and knowledge are concerned, anything goes. A critic's insights and views, and her conscious recognition of their inevitable partiality, do not render her practice identical or even quite similar to highly personal modes of knowing, or efforts of understanding, as exemplified by, say, the practice of confession, or the transferential interchange induced by/in the psychoanalytic situation. In contrast, such critical self-reflexivity more readily resembles the act of bearing witness, of giving an account of oneself in relation to, in this case, cultural events that offer themselves as complex phenomena requiring elucidation. Moreover, insofar as the practice of cultural analysis can be seen, to some extent, as not dissimilar to that of testifying in court, of giving testimony in a public setting about events that somehow or other involve the speaking subject on a personal plane, the cultural analyst speaks from a position that can never be wholly detached from the events themselves. In other words, critical accounts of cultural phenomena can never be disinterested.

Clearly, then, I had a decided interest in showing how mainstream (Hollywood) films, such as Verhoeven's *Basic Instinct* and Polanski's *Bitter Moon*, effectively exploit a collective imaginary in which the lesbian figures as a site of absence or, more precisely, as the abjected underside of a cultural consciousness rooted in structures of power/knowledge that are not only fundamentally phallocratic (and thus misogynist), but also thoroughly lesbophobic in nature. Similarly, though almost conversely, I had a particular interest in attempting to bring to the surface the 'unspoken' lesbian subtexts speaking through and against the ostensibly straightforward surface discourses of pre-liberation, female-authored narrative texts, such as Plath's *The Bell Jar* and Bowen's *Friends and Relations*. By making these lesbian subtexts more widely heard, my aim, in these instances, was to show that configurations of lesbian desire, however muted, obscured and/or transformed they may seem, are nonetheless there to be seen, are manifestly present – if only one has learned how to look for, listen to and recognize them. My efforts at trying to understand the function and significance of configurations of lesbian sexuality in feminist critical and theoretical discourse were, finally, by no means less driven by interest; they found their driving force in a long-standing commitment to a radical feminist project in which I have, over the years, and with varying intensity, invested parts of my self, intellectually, politically as well as emotionally, as a reading/speaking subject and as a lesbian, that is to say, as a subject of knowledge as well as desire.

If called upon to define what these various forms of investment jointly amount to, to describe what ultimately binds these discrete and partial testimonies together, I would point to the possibility and transformational potential of what Mikhail Bakhtin has called 'participative thinking'.[2] That is to say: a practice of thought whose qualifying trait is not its disengagement from the sordid facts of the material reality it seeks to bring under control or master (as in 'objective' scientific practice), but which, on the contrary, constitutes an ongoing activity, comprising a continuous chain of performed and performative acts or deeds in everyday life. Participatory thought is a mode of *un-indifferent* thinking which entails engagement, commitment, involvement, concern, and indeed, *interest*. By provoking such interest, each of the texts examined in these pages have allowed me to engage in such a practice. Simultaneously addressing me as a critical subject and as a psychosexually distinct being-in-the-world, their variously appealing, annoying, even exasperating qualities succeeded in somehow or other arousing my interest. More generally speaking, the cultural texts that make up the material context of our existence as individuals enable us, in our own specific ways, to enter into another scene, or rather, into a scene of Otherness. Only the confrontation with such Otherness empowers us to ask the questions we subsequently find ourselves concerned and, more likely than not, perpetually struggling with. As such, any text could be seen as a 'scene of address', presenting its recipient/addressee with a scene of choices: choices about what questions to ask, about what acts or deeds of thought to perform.[3] Using the excentricity of a lesbian subject-position as a critical source of insight into the hegemonic structures of heterosexual presumption, I have tried, in my own (interested) way, to open another 'scene of address' in order to raise yet other questions about the meanings of lesbianism in the Western cultural imagination. The product of these acts of thought, the book that forms the material result of my 'participation' in the prevailing socio-cultural scene, will, at best, in its turn appeal to, provoke and address its readers. As a performed effort of understanding, it cannot aspire to resolve once and for all any of the questions it raises; at most, it will allow for the generation of further questions.

Bakhtin describes the practitioners of 'participative thinking' as 'those who know how not to detach the performed act from its product'.[4] By bearing witness to the significance of lesbian configurations in the timespace in which I perform my acts as a critic and theorist, as well as by attesting to the interested nature of my participation in the very cultural scene it is my purpose to critique, I try to live up to the challenge entailed by such a conception of 'thinking'. Within a Bakhtinian framework, neither the notion of a 'performed act' nor that of its 'product' can be conceived of in the finite terms of resolution or closure: making up 'an indivisible unity', neither can have meaning outside the 'unitary and unique context of life'.[5] And since the context from which I speak, this thing called 'my life', consists in an ongoing process of recontextualization in relation to a complex range of historically shifting, multiplying scenes of discrete othernesses, my resistance to closure would, in the final analysis, seem entirely appropriate. What is more, as Virginia Woolf clairvoyantly observed nearly seventy years ago, especially where questions of sexuality are concerned, 'one cannot hope to tell the truth'. Considering the unfathomable character of the sexual figure at the centre of my textual investigations, I cannot but leave this quest on a deliberate note of *in*conclusion. For in the end, as Woolf so perceptively remarks, 'one can only hope' that, as a scene of address, the product of one's thinking practice will eventually develop into a scene of choices in its own right. As such, it can do no more than give its 'audience the chance of drawing their own conclusions as they observe the limitations, the prejudices, the idiosyncrasies of the speaker'. By ultimately remaining inconclusive, I hope that my foregoing testimony will succeed in doing precisely that.

Notes

Prologue

1 Cf. Sally Munt, ed., *New Lesbian Criticism: Literary and Cultural Readings* (Hemel Hempstead: Harvester Wheatsheaf, 1992); Teresa de Lauretis, 'Queer Theory; Lesbian and Gay Sexualities, An Introduction', *Differences: A Journal of Feminist Cultural Studies* 5, no. 2 (1991); Domna C. Stanton, Introduction to *Discourses of Sexuality: From Aristotle to AIDS* (Ann Arbor: University of Michigan Press, 1992).
2 Terry Castle, *The Apparitional Lesbian: Female Homosexuality and Modern Culture* (New York: Columbia University Press, 1993), 34.
3 Ibid., 35.
4 See Maaike Meijer, *De Lust tot Lezen: Nederlandse Dichteressen en het Literaire Systeem* (Amsterdam: Sara/van Gennep, 1988).
5 See Steven Seidman, *Romantic Longings: Love in America, 1830–1980* (New York & London: Routledge, 1991), 65–91.

Chapter 1 Defining Differences: The Lavender Menace and *The Color Purple*

1 On the ways in which the dominant media orchestrated and diminished the meaning and influence of the women's movement from the moment of its emergence, see Susan J. Douglas, *Where the Girls Are: Growing up Female with the Mass Media* (1994; reprint, New York: Times Books/Random House, 1995).
2 In another version of the anecdote, Friedan is said to have used the phrase 'lavender herring', a play on the 1950s term 'red herring', a term which, in the context of the Cold War, was used to refer to the 'Communist threat'.

3   Martha Gever and Nathalie Magnan, 'The Same Difference: On Lesbian Representation', in *Stolen Glances: Lesbians Take Photographs*, ed. Tessa Boffin and Jean Fraser (London: Pandora, 1991), 67–75.

4   *The Color Purple*, dir. Steven Spielberg (Amblin Entertainment, USA, 1985). See, for an introduction to feminist film studies as well as a critical appreciation of Spielberg's film, Anneke Smelik, 'What Meets the Eye: Feminist Film Studies', in *Women's Studies and Culture: A Feminist Introduction*, ed. Rosemarie Buikema and Anneke Smelik (London & New Jersey: Zed Books, 1995), 66–81.

5   Cora Kaplan, 'Keeping the Color in *The Color Purple*', in *Sea Changes: Culture and Feminism* (London: Verso, 1986), 177–87; 178.

6   Ibid., 180.

7   Ibid., 180–1.

8   Ibid., 185.

9   Alison Light, 'Fear of the Happy Ending: *The Color Purple*, Reading and Racism', in *Plotting Change: Contemporary Women's Fiction*, ed. Linda Anderson (London, Melbourne, Auckland: Edward Arnold, 1990), 85–96; 92.

10   Ibid., 94; 92.

11   See Bonnie Zimmerman, 'Exiting From Patriarchy: The Lesbian Novel of Development', in *The Voyage In: Fictions of Female Development*, ed. Marianne Hirsch and Elizabeth Langland (Hanover & London: The University Press of New England, 1985), 244–57.

12   Cf. bell hooks, 'Writing the Subject: Reading *The Color Purple*', in *Reading Black, Reading Feminist: A Critical Anthology*, ed. Henry Louis Gates Jr (New York: Meridian, 1990), 454–70.

13   hooks, in fact, begins her characteristically provocative, yet somewhat erratic, argument by defining *The Color Purple* as a 'narrative of "sexual confession"', that eventually does not fulfil its radical potential in that Walker, 'unable to reconcile sexuality and power, replaces the longing for sexual pleasure with an erotic metaphysic animated by a vision of the unity of all things'. Ibid., 460.

14   See further on this subject bell hooks, 'Homophobia in Black Communities', in *Talking Back: Thinking Feminist, Thinking Black* (Boston: South End Press, 1989), 120–6.

15   On the emergence and historical significance of this by now stereotypical figure, see Esther Newton, 'The Mythic Mannish Lesbian: Radclyffe Hall and the New Woman', in *Hidden from History: Reclaiming the Gay and Lesbian Past*, ed. Martin Bauml Duberman, Martha Vicinus and George Chauncey Jr (London: Penguin, 1987), 281-93; Carol Smith-Rosenberg, 'The New Woman as Androgyne: Social Disorder and Gender Crisis 1870–1936', in *Disorderly Conduct: Visions of Gender in Victorian America* (New York: Oxford University Press, 1985), 245–96. For a psychoanalytic reading of the figure, see Teresa de Lauretis, 'Perverse Desire: The Lure of the Mannish Lesbian', *Australian Feminist Studies* 13 (1991), 15–26, which is further developed in chapter 5, 'The Lure of the Mannish Lesbian: The Fantasy of Castration and the Signification of Desire', in *The Practice of Love: Lesbian Sexuality and*

Perverse Desire (Bloomington & Indianapolis: Indiana University Press, 1994), 203–53.

16 Light, 'Fear of the Happy Ending', 93.

Chapter 2   *Basic Instinct:* The Lesbian Spectre as Castrating Agent

1 Among the most prominent early sexologists (medical men who, in line with prevailing scientific assumptions, sought to classify, define, and describe so-called abnormal or deviant patterns of sexual behaviour in terms of sickness rather than as sin), were Havelock Ellis, Casper, and Krafft-Ebing. Famous examples of sexologists' studies are Havelock Ellis, *Studies in the Psychology of Sex* (New York: Random House, 1936); Richard von Krafft-Ebing, *Psychopathia Sexualis with Especial Reference to the Antipathic Sexual Instincts*, tr. F. J. Rebman (Stuttgart: 1886; reprint, Brooklyn: Physicians and Surgeons Books Co., 1908). On the influence of these and Freud's theories of sexual deviancy, see George Chauncey Jr, 'From Sexual Inversion to Homosexuality: Medicine and the Changing Conceptions of Female Deviance', *Salmagundi* 68–9 (Fall 1982/Winter 1983), 114–46. For a brief overview of the development of sexological thought, see Gert Hekma, 'A History of Sexology: Social and Historical Aspects of Sexuality', in *From Sappho to De Sade: Moments in the History of Sexuality*, ed, Jan Bremmer (London: Routledge, 1989), 173–93. A thoughtful account of the effect of the European sexologists' discourse on the lives of American women at the end of the 19th and in the early 20th century, is given by Lilian Faderman, *Odd Girls and Twilight Lovers: A History of Lesbian Life in Twentieth-Century America* (New York: Columbia University Press, 1991).

2 Freud found himself so much at a loss with his two 'female homosexual' patients that he left both analyses unconcluded and the respective case histories riddled with internal contradictions. These were the so-called 'Dora case' ('Fragment of an Analysis of a Case of Hysteria', in *Case Histories I: 'Dora' and 'Little Hans'*, ed. Angela Richards, tr. James Strachey, Pelican Freud Library, vol. 8 (Harmondsworth: Penguin, 1977)); and 'The Psychogenesis of a Case of Homosexuality in a Woman', in *Case Histories II: 'Rat Man', Schreber, 'Wolf Man', Female Homosexuality*, ed. Angela Richards, tr. James Strachey, Pelican Freud Library, vol. 9 (Harmondsworth: Penguin, 1987).

3 Teresa de Lauretis, 'Sexual Indifference and Lesbian Representation', *Theatre Journal* 5 (1988), 155–77; 156.

4 Sara Hoagland, 'Lesbian Epistemology' (1978), unpublished paper cited in Marilyn Frye, 'To Be and Be Seen: The Politics of Reality', in *The Politics of Reality: Essays in Feminist Theory* (Trumansberg, NY: The Crossing Press, 1983), 152.

5 Ibid., 162

6 For a concise introduction to Bakhtin's life and thought, see Katerina Clark and Michael Holquist, *Mikhail Bakhtin* (Cambridge: Belknap Press of Harvard University, 1984). Michael F. Bernard-Douglas, *Mikhail Bakhtin: Between Phenomenology and Marxism* (Cambridge: Cambridge University Press, 1994) offers an interesting critique on the 'usefulness' of Bakhtinian thought in the context of a materialist literary critical practice.

7 Lynda Hart, 'Why The Woman Did It: *Basic Instinct* and Its Vicissitudes', in *Fatal Women: Lesbian Sexuality and the Mark of Aggression* (Princeton: Princeton University Press, 1994), 125

8 See, e.g., Jane Gallop, *Feminism and Psychoanalysis: The Daughter's Seduction* (Ithaca and London: Cornell University Press and Macmillan, 1982), 113–31; and Julia Kristeva, 'Motherhood According to Bellini', in *Desire in Language: A Semiotic Approach to Literature and Art*, ed. Léon Roudiez, tr. Alice Jardine, Thomas Gora, and Léon Roudiez (Oxford: Blackwell, 1980).

9 Hart also points to the 'doubling effect' that determines the visual representation of *Basic Instinct*'s main female characters, a conventional pattern of imagery that is 'characteristic of the lesbian as autoerotic/narcissistic', ibid. 129. In my discussion of Sylvia Plath's *The Bell Jar* in chapter 4, I offer a more detailed discussion of the related phenomena of psychic and literary 'doubling' in the haunting figure of (repressed) lesbian desire.

10 Camilla Griggers, 'Phantom and Reel Projections: Lesbians and the (Serial) Killing Machine', in *Posthuman Bodies*, ed. Judith Halberstam and Ira Livingston (Bloomington and Indianapolis: Indiana University Press, 1995), 162–76; 166.

11 Ibid.

12 Teresa de Lauretis introduced the cinematographic term 'space-off' into feminist theory in order to designate the 'movement from the space represented by/in a representation, by/in a discourse, by/in a sex-gender system, to the space not represented, yet implied (unseen) in them', in 'The Technology of Gender', in *Technologies of Gender: Essays on Theory, Film and Fiction* (Bloomington & Indianapolis: Indiana University Press, 1987), 26.

13 Jean Laplanche and Jean-Bertrand Pontalis, *The Language of Psychoanalysis*, tr. Donald Nicholson-Smith (London: Karnac Books and the Institute of Psycho-Analysis, 1988), 335. See Sigmund Freud, 'Wolf Man', in *Case Histories II*, 233–345.

14 'Hom(m)osexuality', a term coined by Luce Irigaray, is a diacritical pun on the French words *homme* (man) and the Greek *homos* (same). It serves to indicate that patriarchal culture is an economy of the Same, in which the strongest and most powerful bonds are those among men, and in which the female Other merely functions as the object of male exchange. See Luce Irigaray, 'Commodities Among Themselves', in *This Sex Which Is Not One*, tr. Catherine Porter and Carolyn Burke (Ithaca: Cornell University Press, 1985), 192–7.

15 The film's markedly ambivalent ending has given rise to considerable critical dissension. While some have proposed that Tramell and not

Gardner is the 'real' murderess in *Basic Instinct*, I take the closing scene to signal that the castration anxiety posed by the figure of the lesbian cannot be resolved by the elimination of individual lesbians. The appearance of the castrating ice-pick under the bed hence conveys that such anxiety endures precisely because phallocentric ideology ensures its inscription in the male subject's psyche. Hart's reading, though first and foremost stipulating the critical function of the 'doubling effect' in the fantasmatic representation of lesbianism in mainstream cinema, and thus insisting on the indivisibility of the two characters/culprits, most closely resembles my own, see Hart 'Why The Woman Did It', 132–4. An alternative reading is provided by Angela Galvin, '*Basic Instinct*: Damning Dykes', in *The Good, the Bad and the Gorgeous: Popular Culture's Romance with Lesbianism*, ed. Diane Hamer and Belinda Budge (London: Pandora, 1994), 218–31.

16   Judith Butler, 'Imitation and Gender Insubordination', in *Inside/Out: Lesbian Theories, Gay Theories*, ed. Diana Fuss (New York: Routledge, 1991), 13–31; 20.

17   See Monique Wittig, 'On the Social Contract', in *The Straight Mind and Other Essays* (Boston: Beacon Press, 1992), 33–45.

18   Butler, 'Imitation and Gender Insubordination', 20.

19   Ibid., 21. Butler loosely paraphrases Esther Newton's line of argument in *Mother's Camp: Female Impersonators in America* (Chicago: University of Chicago Press, 1972).

Chapter 3   Impossible Subject among Multiple Cross-overs: Roman Polanski's *Bitter Moon*

1   For theoretical explorations of the phenomenon of multiple boundary-crossing from a lesbian perspective see 'Recasting the Primal Scene: Film and Lesbian Representation,' 81–148, and 'The Lure of the Mannish Lesbian,' 203–56, in de Lauretis, *The Practice of Love*; 'Slash and Suture: The Border's Figuration of Colonialism, Phallocentrism, and Homophobia in *Borderlands/La Frontera: The New Mesiza*,' in Annamarie Jagose, *Lesbian Utopics* (New York: Routledge, 1994), 137–58; 'Passing Queering: Nella Larsen's Psychoanalytic Challenge,' 167–86, and 'Gender Is Burning: Questions of Appropriation and Subversion,' 121–42, in Judith Butler, *Bodies That Matter: On the Discursive Limits of 'Sex'* (New York: Routledge, 1994); 'Race and Reproduction: *Single* White *Female*', 104–23, in Lynda Hart, *Fatal Women*; Judith Raiskin, 'Inverts and Hybrids: Lesbian Rewritings of Sexual and Racial Identities', in *The Lesbian Postmodern*, ed. Laura Doan (New York: Columbia University Press, 1994), 156–72.

2   For illuminating discussions of these films, see the chapters 'Chloe liked Olivia: Death, Desire, and Detection in the Female Buddy Film', 65–88, and 'Race and Reproduction: *Single* White *Female*', 104–23, in Hart, *Fatal Women*.

3 Single-author books, such as those by Judith Roof, *A Lure of Knowledge: Lesbian Sexuality and Theory* (New York: Columbia University Press, 1991); de Lauretis, *The Practice of Love*; Butler, *Bodies that Matter*; Hart, *Fatal Women*, all contain chapters on popular cultural forms. Examples of critical anthologies exclusively devoted to popular cultural production in relation to lesbianism, are Gabriele Griffin, ed., *Outwrite: Lesbianism and Popular Culture* (London: Pluto Press, 1993); Arlene Stein, ed., *Sisters, Sexperts, Queens: Beyond the Lesbian Nation* (New York: Plume, 1993); Laura Doan, ed., *The Lesbian Postmodern*; Liz Gibbs, ed., *Daring to Dissent: Lesbian Culture from Margin to Mainstream* (London: Cassell, 1994); Diane Hamer and Belinda Budge, eds, *The Good, the Bad and the Gorgeous*.

4 Cathy Griggers, 'Lesbian Bodies in the Age of (Post)Mechanical Reproduction,' in *The Lesbian Postmodern*, ed. Doan, 118–34; 119.

5 Ibid.

6 Cf. Butler, 'Imitation and Gender Insubordination', in *Inside/Out: Lesbian Theories, Gay Theories*.

7 On the persistently 'haunting' presence of the lesbian in the margins of the Eurowestern cultural imagination, see Terry Castle, *The Apparitional Lesbian*.

8 See, for instance, Hamer and Budge, *The Good, the Bad and the Gorgeous*.

9 Milou van Rossum, 'Zin in een vriendin', *Glow*, summer special of the Dutch *Avant Garde* (August 1993), 58–61.

Chapter 4 Sex/textual Conflicts in *The Bell Jar*: Sylvia Plath's Doubling Negatives

1 Sylvia Plath, *The Bell Jar* (1963; reprint, London: Faber & Faber, 1980). Subsequent page references are to this edition and will appear in parentheses in the text.

2 'The story of Sylvia Plath' continues to vex as much as to fascinate her various biographers' imaginations. Plath's life has been the subject of two recent major biographies written by women (Linda Wagner-Martin, *Sylvia Plath: A Biography* (London and New York: Simon & Schuster, 1987) and Anne Stevenson, *Bitter Fame: A Life of Sylvia Plath* (Boston: Houghton Mifflin, 1989)), whereas her death – significantly – forms the primary focus of a male attempt to capture the author's life narrative (Ronald Hayman, *The Death and Life of Sylvia Plath* (London: Minerva, 1991)) – a shift in emphasis which, incidentally, gives new impetus to the question of the gendered significance of beginnings and endings of stories. Cf. Teresa de Lauretis, 'Desire in Narrative', in *Alice Doesn't: Feminism, Semiotics, Cinema* (Bloomington: Indiana University Press, 1988). Wagner-Martin presents an appreciative though conventional account of Plath's life; unfortunately, her reading of *The*

Bell Jar in this volume seems more informed by wishful thinking than by careful attention to the contradictions in the text. Her later work, *The Bell Jar: A Novel of the Fifties* (New York: Twayne, 1992) presents a more persuasive analysis. Stevenson's is a particularly disturbing book, since its author evidently has little sympathy for the character she is trying to reconstruct. The 'bitterness' of the book's title, in fact, suggests more about the biographer's relationship to her subject than about that subject itself.

3   For extensive critical material, consult Gary Lane and Maria Stevens, *Sylvia Plath: A Bibliography* (Metuchen, NJ: Scarecrow, 1978). A slightly dated list of works by and about the author is provided by Stephen Tabor, *Sylvia Plath: An Analytic Bibliography* (London & New York: Mansell Publishing, 1986). For additional essays, see Edward Butscher, ed., *Sylvia Plath: The Woman and the Work* (New York: Dodd, Mead, & Co., 1977); Gary Lane, ed., *Sylvia Plath: New Views on the Poetry* (Baltimore: Johns Hopkins Press, 1979); Paul Alexander, ed., *Ariel Ascending: Writings about Sylvia Plath* (New York: Harper & Row, 1984); Linda W. Wagner, ed., *Critical Essays on Sylvia Plath* (Boston: G. K. Hall, 1984).

4   Examples of this line of argument are Ellen Moers, *Literary Women* (1963; reprint, London: Women's Press, 1978); Elaine Showalter, *A Literature of Their Own: British Women Novelists From Brontë to Lessing* (1977; reprint, London: Virago, 1978); Annis Pratt, *Archetypal Patterns in Women's Fiction* (Brighton: Harvester, 1981); Rosalind Miles, *The Female Form: Women Writers and the Conquest of the Novel* (London: Routledge, 1990). Jacqueline Rose, *The Haunting of Sylvia Plath* (London: Verso, 1991) is the most thoughtful and illuminating feminist study of Plath's life and work to date.

5   See, for instance, Elaine Martin, 'Mothers, Madness, and the Middle Class in *The Bell Jar* and *Les Mots pour le Dire*', *French-American Review* 5 (Spring 1981), 24–47; Barbara White, *Growing Up Female: Adolescent Girlhood in American Fiction* (Westport & London, 1985); Linda W. Wagner, 'Plath's *The Bell Jar* as Female Bildungsroman', *Women's Studies* 12 (1983), 55–68.

6   Betty Friedan, *The Feminine Mystique* (New York: Norton, 1963).

7   Peter Conn, *The Cambridge Illustrated History of American Literature* (London & New York: Guild Publishing, 1990), 481.

8   Wagner-Martin, *Sylvia Plath*, 187.

9   Sylvia Plath, *Letters Home: Correspondence 1950–1963* (New York: Harper & Row, 1975); Sylvia Plath, *The Journals of Sylvia Plath* (New York: Ballantine, 1983).

10   Wagner-Martin, *Sylvia Plath*, 186; 189.

11   Stevenson, *Bitter Fame*, 285; 227.

12   Wagner-Martin, *Sylvia Plath*, 186.

13   Elaine Marks traces the development of model of the 'unequal couple' from its origins in Greek myth to its contemporary survival in lesbian utopian fiction in her essay 'Lesbian Intertextuality,' in *Homosexualities and French Literature*, ed. Elaine Marks and George Stambolian

(Ithaca: Cornell University Press, 1979), 353–77. I will have occasion to explore this model in more detail in chapter 5.

14 Cf. Wagner-Martin, *Sylvia Plath*, 186–91.

15 The phrase 'transposed autobiography' derives from Elizabeth Bowen, who, having first used it in a very restricted sense, eventually expanded the notion to encompass fiction in general. See Elizabeth Bowen, 'Preface to *Stories by Elizabeth Bowen*', in *Afterthought* (London: Longmans, 1962), 78.

16 Cited in Stevenson, *Bitter Fame*, 285.

17 See, in addition to Stevenson's and Wagner-Martin's accounts of the novel's reception, Pat MacPherson, *Reflecting on The Bell Jar* (London & New York: Routledge, 1991).

18 Gérard Genette, *Narrative Discourse*, trans. Jane Lewin (Oxford: Basil Blackwell, 1986). Wallace Martin explains these terms under two different headings. He describes diegesis as an 'element of narration', comparable to summary or 'telling', and applicable when a 'narrator describes what happened in his/her own words (or recounts what characters think and feel, without quotation).' In this scheme the extradiegetic level falls under the category of 'authorial narration', indicating whether a narrator is her/himself 'inside' or 'outside' the story s/he narrates. See Wallace Martin, *Recent Theories of Narrative* (Ithaca & London: Cornell University Press, 1986), 124; 135. Shlomith Rimmon-Kenan defines diegesis as the narrative 'events themselves', while the extradiegetic level refers to the 'highest level' within the hierarchy of narratives within narratives characteristic of novelistic discourse, i.e., the one 'immediately superior to the first narrative and concerned with its narration'. See Shlomith Rimmon-Kenan, *Narrative Fiction: Contemporary Poetics* (London: Methuen, 1983), 91. I will be using the terms in the latter sense. Susan Sniader-Lanser further distinguishes the 'extra-fictional voice' to designate the authorial instance, who/which, though 'absent' from the narrative text, is always present as the 'most direct counterpart for the historical author'. Cf. Susan Sniader-Lanser, *The Narrative Act: Point of View in Prose Fiction* (Princeton: Princeton University Press, 1981), 123.

19 The useful phrase 'configurations of lesbian sexuality' I have shamelessly appropriated from Roof, who, to my knowledge, first used it in *A Lure of Knowledge*.

20 Ibid., 5.

21 Ibid.

22 Irigaray, 'Commodities Among Themselves.' See also chapter 2, note 10.

23 I borrow the term 'complificating' from Meijer, who coined its Dutch equivalent in *De Lust tot Lezen*.

24 Roof, *A Lure of Knowledge*, 5, 4. On the significance and function of masks and signals as textual strategies in (male) homosex/textualities, see, for instance, Marita Keilson-Lauritz, 'Maske und Signal: Textstrategien der Homoerotik', in *Homosexualitäten-Literarisch: Literaturwissenschaftliche Beiträge zum Internationalen Kongress*

'*Homosexuality which Homosexuality? Amsterdam 1987*', ed. Maria Kalveram and Wolfgang Popp (Essen: Verlag Die Blaue Eule, 1991), 63–75; on lesbian masks in Dutch literature of the 1950s, see Pattynama, 'Maskering en Geheimhouding', in *Schrijfsters in de Jaren Vijftig*, ed. Margriet Prinssen and Lucie Th. Vermeij (Amsterdam: An Dekker, 1990), 252–63.

25 Katherine Dalsimer, *Female Adolescence: Psychoanalytic Reflections on Literature* (New Haven & London: Yale University Press, 1986), 4.

26 For bibliographical references, see chapter 2, note 1.

27 Despite its gender bias, and its heterocentrism – occasionally bordering on acute homophobia – Erik Erikson, *Identity: Youth and Crisis* (London: Faber & Faber, 1968) remains one of the seminal studies of the phenomenon of (male) adolescence in modern Western culture.

28 Michel Foucault, 'Technologies of the Self,' in *Technologies of the Self: A Seminar with Michel Foucault*, ed. Luther H. Martin, Huck Gutman and Patrick H. Hutton (Amherst: University of Massachusetts Press, 1988), 16–49.

29 On the ways in which this initially 18th-century – predominantly male – genre was transformed, at the end of the 19th and throughout the 20th century into the specifically female genre of the 'novel of awakening', see Abel, Hirsch and Langland, eds, *The Voyage In*. In my *Elizabeth Bowen: A Reputation in Writing* (New York: New York University Press, 1994), I pay considerable attention to the interrelations between lesbian desire and adolescence in literary texts. For an extensive study of female adolescence in contemporary fiction, see further Pamela Pattynama, *Passages: Vrouwelijke Adolescentie als Verhaal en Vertoog* (Kampen: Kok Agora, 1992); or, in the context of American literature only, White, *Growing Up Female*.

30 As Plath's various biographers contend, and her own *Journals* confirm, the author-poet was herself quite literally split apart by the double standard informing the myth of femininity prevailing in her life-time.

31 Julia Kristeva, 'The Adolescent Novel,' in *Abjection, Melancholia, and Love: The Work of Julia Kristeva*, ed. John Fletcher and Andrew Benjamin (London & New York: Routledge, 1990).

32 Ibid., 9; 10.

33 Ibid., 20.

34 Kaja Silverman, *The Acoustic Mirror: The Female Voice in Psychoanalysis and Cinema* (Bloomington & Indianapolis: Routledge, 1988), 122.

35 For a general introduction to postmodernism, see, for instance, Linda Hutcheon, *A Poetics of Postmodernism: History, Theory, Fiction* (New York & London: Routledge, 1988); for an appreciation of the postmodern phenomenon in the context of lesbian sexuality, see Doan, ed., *The Lesbian Postmodern*; and also, Sally Munt, 'Somewhere Over the Rainbow ... Postmodernism and the Fiction of Sarah Schulman', in *New Lesbian Criticism*, ed. Munt, 33–50. With the terms 'heteroglossia' and 'carnival' I am loosely referring to the work of Mikhail Bakhtin. A

comprehensive introduction to his work and thought is provided by
Clark and Holquist, *Mikhail Bakhtin*.

36 Douglas, *Where the Girls Are*, 99.
37 Ibid., 100.
38 MacPherson, *Reflecting on The Bell Jar*, 3.
39 This was Hoover's term for American Communists.
40 The term 'ideological state apparatus' derives from the French political
    scientist Louis Althusser. On the different functions and effects of
    'Repressive State Apparatuses', e.g., the police and the legal system, as
    distinct from 'Ideological State Apparatuses', e.g., the educational sys-
    tem, the family, the church, and the mass media, see Louis Althusser,
    'Ideology and Ideological State Apparatuses (Notes Towards an
    Investigation)', in *Essays on Ideology* (1970; reprint, London: Verso,
    1984), 1–60.
41 MacPherson, *Reflecting on The Bell Jar*, 3.
42 Katie King, 'Audre Lorde's Lacquered Layerings: The Lesbian Bar as a
    Site of Literary Production', in *New Lesbian Criticism*, ed. Munt, 51–74;
    52. Jonathan Katz has extensively documented the 'simultaneous perse-
    cution of "perverts" and "subversives"' taking place in the US from
    1950–5. Cf. Jonathan Katz, *Gay American History: Lesbians and Gay
    Men in the U.S.A.* (1976; reprint, New York: Avon, 1978), 91.
43 Robert Rogers, *A Psychoanalytic Study of the Double in Literature*
    (Detroit: Wayne State University Press, 1970), 4.
44 Ibid., 5.
45 Ibid., 13.
46 Ibid.
47 See, for example, Frank W. Putnam, *Diagnosis & Treatment of Multiple
    Personality Disorder* (New York & London: The Guildford Press,
    1989); Barry M. Cohen et al. eds, *Multiple Personality Disorder from the
    Inside Out* (Baltimore: The Sylvan Press, 1991). The Dutch documen-
    tary film *De Ontkenning* (1992) (*Denial*) offers a careful and authentic
    portrait of a young woman suffering from MPD, shedding a disturbing
    light on the ramifications and backgrounds of the disorder.
48 Rogers, *A Psychoanalytic Study*, 6.
49 See Erikson, *Identity: Youth and Crisis*, 128.
50 The racial connotations of the interconnected patterns of imagery
    (black/white; negative/positive) sustained throughout the text are never
    explicitly addressed in those terms. Considering the growing promi-
    nence of the 'race question' in US politics and society in the late 1950s
    and early 1960s, they cannot, however, but be considered powerful
    echoes as they speak through the protagonist's anxious self-searching
    questions. See Wini Breines, *Young, White, and Miserable: Growing Up
    Female in the Fifties* (Boston: Beacon Press, 1992), for an exploration of
    The Bell Jar's racial subtext.
51 In the Old Testament, Esther is a beautiful Jewess who becomes queen
    of Persia and saves her people from a massacre. The protagonist's
    Christian name hence suggests strong (Jewish) womanhood, and further
    reinforces her identification with Ethel Rosenberg. This given name at

the same time sits in sharp contrast with her family name (the Name of the Father), Greenwood, which at once signifies 'immaturity' and 'confusion' (as in being 'in the woods' about a problem or question).

52 See Newton, 'The Mythic Mannish Lesbian'; de Lauretis, 'Perverse Desire'.

53 Wagner-Martin's comment on this passage provides a perfect example of the strategies of erasure commonly practised on configurations of lesbian sexuality. While she may well be correct in maintaining that 'for Esther ... the suspicion of her friend's sexual preference is much less important than the fact of her death', she fails either to perceive or acknowledge that it is precisely because of her 'sexual preference' that Joan's death acquires such crucial importance for Esther. See Wagner-Martin, *Sylvia Plath*, 187.

Chapter 5   Queer Undercurrents: Disruptive Desire in Elizabeth Bowen's *Friends and Relations*

1 Cf. Shari Benstock, 'Expatriate Sapphic Modernism: Entering Literary History', in *Lesbian Texts and Contexts: Radical Revisions*, ed. Karla Jay and Joanne Glasgow (New York: New York University Press, 1990), 183–203.

2 The first to situate Bowen in a tradition of lesbian writing was the American/Canadian novelist Jane Rule, who included a short essay entitled 'Elizabeth Bowen', in *Lesbian Images* (Freedom, Calif.: The Crossing Press, 1975). My own earlier work forms, as far as I know, the first extended effort at reassessing the author's accomplishment from a poststructuralist lesbian feminist perspective. See hoogland, 'From Marginality to Ex-Centricity Feminist Critical Theory and the Case of Elizabeth Bowen', Ph.D. diss., University of Amsterdam, 1991; and, *Elizabeth Bowen*.

3 For an extensive historical overview of early 20th-century female writing practices with special – though sometimes disturbing – reference to lesbianism, see Shari Benstock, *Women of the Left Bank: Paris, 1900–1940* (Austin: University of Texas Press, 1986).

4 I here hesitantly endorse Benstock's use of the term 'Sapphic modernism', in Benstock, 'Expatriate Sapphic Modernism'.

5 Elizabeth Bowen, *Friends and Relations* (1931; reprint, Harmondsworth: Penguin, 1982).

6 Benstock, 'Expatriate Sapphic Modernism', 184–5.

7 As mentioned in an earlier chapter, Barbara Smith has argued with reference to Alice Walker's novel *Sula* that such a critique of heterosexual institutions, in tandem with a concentration on female same-sex relations, sufficiently qualifies a text as a 'lesbian' one. See Smith, 'Toward a Black Feminist Criticism.' Although I would contest this claim in its generality (there are, after all, innumerable novels that severely criticize heterosexual relations without undermining or even questioning the

legitimacy of the heterosexual norm, let alone allowing for the alternative of same-sex desire – as distinct from female friendship or bonding), I would maintain that, in conjunction with other, more direct inscriptions of non-normative desire, such critiques can and do signify lesbian sexuality in a substantial number of pre-1968 female fictional writings. Jane Rule, in the essay referred to above, also points to Bowen's insistently bleak representation of heterosexual relations, and concomitant privileging of the relationships among a variety of female characters (Rule, 'Elizabeth Bowen,' 115). See for further discussion of this question my concluding chapter, 'From Marginality to Ex-Centricity,' 291–312, in *Elizabeth Bowen*.

8   Victoria Glendinning, *Elizabeth Bowen: A Portrait of a Writer* (1977; reprint, Harmondsworth: Penguin, 1985), 75.

9   Derek Verschoyle, *The English Novelists: A Survey of the Novel by Twenty Contemporary Novelists* (London: Chatto and Windus, 1936).

10   The Second World War and its dislocations caused a break in Bowen's novelistic career, creating a lapse which was to last almost eleven years. Whereas she continued publishing throughout the 1940s, it was not until 1949 that she was able to finish the novel dealing with this bewildering historical period, *The Heat of the Day*. In the 1950s and 1960s, her earlier fame and influence went into steady decline. While still enjoying distinct celebrity, Bowen's later novels were critically less well received, still less appreciated by her original fans. In some respects showing a radical departure from her accustomed style and manner, the last two works in particular disappointed many by deviating markedly from what had come to be expected of the 'typical' Bowen novel.

11   An inevitability that, according to Brooke, obliged her to 'deliberately confine herself . . . to the themes which she feels to be safely within her range as a woman novelist', this early male critic gives the impression that it is in effect her sex that he admires most about 'Miss Bowen', or rather, the way she handled the 'limitations and specific advantages of her femininity'. In his view, the author distinguished herself favourably from 'many women novelists' who have 'too boldly . . . ignored the limitations which (whether they like it or not) are implied by the mere fact of being female.' See Jocelyn Brooke, *Elizabeth Bowen*, Supplement to *British Book News*, no. 28 (London: Longmans, 1951), 30.

12   Douglas Hewitt, *English Fiction of the Early Modern Period 1890–1940* (London: Longmans, 1988), 198.

13   Ibid., 196–7.

14   Miles, *The Female Form*, 30.

15   See Hermione Lee, *Elizabeth Bowen: An Estimation* (London & Totowa: Vision/Barnes and Noble, 1981); Glendinning, *Elizabeth Bowen*.

16   These criticisms, incidentally, often arise in connection with repeated, equally disparaging references to the author's evident preoccupation with the theme of female adolescence – a phenomenon still commonly

associated with immaturity, pre-adulthood, 'girlishness', and, last but not least, lesbianism. Cf. my Introduction to *Elizabeth Bowen*, 1–23.

17   'Masculism' is a term developed within feminist criticism, used to designate 'old-fashioned humanism, which considers the study of woman to be a special interest and defines women in terms of man'. Cf. Gayatri Chakravorty Spivak, 'Explanation and Culture: Marginalia', in *In Other Worlds: Essays in Cultural Politics* (Routledge: New York, 1988), 103–17; 283 n. 9.

18   Hewitt, *English Fiction*, 192.

19   While I am not the only critic nor the first to have sought to bring Bowen back into the limelight, few critics have done so by approaching her work from a feminist perspective. To my knowledge, the only other explicitly feminist reading of Bowen's novels is Phyllis Lassner's brief and somewhat superficial *Elizabeth Bowen* (London: Macmillan Education, 1990). Although Lee (*Elizabeth Bowen*) pays considerable attention to the operations of sexual difference in the author's texts, she herself does not assume a feminist critical stance.

20   Bowen, *Friends and Relations*, all page references appearing in parentheses in the text are to the Penguin edition.

21   The narratological term 'focalization', originally introduced by Gérard Genette, refers to the relation between the angle of vision through which narrative events are mediated – including its cognitive, emotive and ideological orientation – and the events themselves. The term is preferable to more traditional ones, such as 'perspective' or 'point of view', in that it enables the theoretical necessity of distinguishing between speaking and seeing, narration and focalizing. Cf. Mieke Bal, *Narratologie: Essais sur la Signification Narrative dans Quatre Romans Modernes* (Paris: Klinksieck, 1977); Rimmon-Kenan, *Narrative Fiction: Contemporary Poetics*.

22   Elizabeth Bowen, 'Notes on Writing a Novel', in *Pictures and Conversations*, ed. Spencer Curtis Brown (London: Allen Lane, 1975), 177.

23   Women in England had to wait till after the First World War to finally gain the right to vote. In 1918, general suffrage was granted to all men of 21 and older, while women had to grow to the mature age of 30 to warrant the same 'privilege'. It was only in 1928 that the required age for female voters was equally lowered to 21. Bowen, having earned her own living from her early twenties, hence acquired this formal token of full citizenship at the age of 29.

24   Cf. hoogland, *Elizabeth Bowen*, 24–106.

25   Marks, 'Lesbian Intertextuality'.

26   Castle, *The Apparitional Lesbian*, 85. See also Meijer, *De Lust tot Lezen*; Pamela Pattynama, 'De Herinnering aan het Oude Verhaal' (Old Stories Remembered), *Lover* 2 (1989), 88–92; Bonnie Zimmerman, 'What Has Never Been: An Overview of Lesbian Feminist Criticism', in *Making a Difference: Feminist Literary Criticism*, ed. Gayle Green and Coppèlia Kahn (London: Methuen, 1985), 177–210.

27   To name but a few examples that readily spring to mind: Antonia

White's *Frost in May* (1933); Lillian Helman's notorious play *The Children's Hour* (1934); Muriel Spark's *The Prime of Miss Jean Brodie* (1961); Rosemary Manning's *The Chinese Garden* (1962); Brigid Brophy's *The Finishing School* (1963), and more recently, Rita Mae Brown's *Ruby Fruit Jungle* (1973), and Elizabeth Jolley's *Foxybaby* (1985).

28 Interview, Elizabeth Bowen and Jocelyn Brooke, 'Broadcast transcribed from a telediphone recording 3rd October 1950', MS (Harry Ransom Humanities Center, University of Texas at Austin).

29 Elizabeth Bowen, *Pictures and Conversations: Chapters of an Autobiography with Other Collected Writings*, ed. Spencer Curtis Brown (London: Allen Lane, 1975), 27.

30 In her reading of this passage, Lee fails to take into account the shifts in focalization, and hence assumes these thoughts are the author-narrator's rather than Lady Elfrida's. Thus missing the irony which is implicitly shed on the focalizing character, Lee uncritically falls in with these sentiments' anxious momentum, and furthermore reveals her own lesbophobia by asserting that Theodora has grown into a 'ghoulish lesbian'. See Lee, *Elizabeth Bowen*, 65.

31 Bowen, *Pictures and Conversations*, 42.

Chapter 6   Fatal Attractions: Feminist Theory and the Lesbian Lure

1 My circumspection in drawing a clear line dividing fiction from non-fiction derives from my belief that the difference between them is one of degree rather than kind. To recall a phrase of Bowen's cited in an earlier chapter, any form of writing is, I think, at however many removes, bound to be 'transposed autobiography'. Bowen, 'Preface to *Stories by Elizabeth Bowen*', 78.

2 I am especially indebted to chapter 5, 'All Analogies Are Faulty: The Fear of Intimacy in Feminist Criticism', 216–36, in Roof, *A Lure of Knowledge*.

3 Roof concentrates her discussion on three feminist anthologies, Elaine Showalter, ed., *The New Feminist Criticism: Essays on Women, Literature, Theory* (New York: Pantheon, 1985); Judith Newton and Deborah Rosenfelt, eds, *Feminist Criticisms and Social Change: Sex, Race and Class in Literature and Culture* (New York: Methuen, 1985); Greene and Kahn, eds, *Making a Difference: Feminist Literary Criticism*. She also, though less extensively, considers Shari Benstock, ed., *Feminist Issues in Literary Scholarship* (Bloomington: Indiana University Press, 1987); Teresa de Lauretis, ed., *Feminist Studies/Critical Studies* (Bloomington: Indiana University Press, 1986); and Bella Brodski and Celeste Schenck, eds, *Life/lines: Theorizing Women's Autobiography* (Ithaca: Cornell University Press, 1988).

4 Roof, *A Lure of Knowledge*, 223.

5   Ibid., 224.
6   Ibid., 217. That the lesbian is particularly amenable to such troping as would underline the figure's irresistibility may be clear from de Lauretis' use of exactly the same term in the title of her essay, 'Perverse Desire: The Lure of the Mannish Lesbian' (1991), later to reappear in the chapter title 'The Lure of the Mannish Lesbian: The Fantasy of Castration and the Signification of Desire', 203–53, in *The Practice of Love*.
7   Roof, *A Lure of Knowledge*, 225.
8   Ibid., 230.
9   Ibid.
10 Ibid., 233.
11 Michèle Barrett and Anne Phillips, eds, *Destabilizing Theory: Contemporary Feminist Debates* (Cambridge: Polity Press, 1992).
12 Roof, *A Lure of Knowledge*, 230.
13 Barrett and Phillips, *Destabilizing Theory*, 4–5.
14 Georges Dubuy and Michelle Perrot, eds, *Histoire des Femmes en Occident*, 5 vols (Paris, 1991–2). The English translation has appeared under the general title *A History of Women in the West*, 5 vols (Cambridge: Harvard University Press 1992–5).
15 Dorelies Kraakman, 'Vijf Maal Nul Is Nul', in *Deugd en Ondeugd: Jaarboek voor Vrouwengeschiedenis* (Amsterdam: Stichting Beheer IISG, 1993), 137–47.
16 Frye, 'To Be and Be Seen', 162.
17 Gayatri Chakravorty Spivak, 'French Feminism in an International Frame', in *In Other Worlds*, 134–53; 149.
18 Jane Gallop, *Around 1981: Academic Feminist Literary Theory* (New York: Routledge, 1992), 7.
19 Although by no means exhaustive, nor even intended to be exactly representative, the selected examples of feminist critical theory and practice discussed above together present a sufficiently 'typical' reflection of the ways in which the subject of lesbianism still generally (con)figures in mainstream feminist thought.
20 Gallop, *Around 1981*, 177–205.
21 Gallop draws on by now 'classic' anthologies, such as Showalter, *The New Feminist Criticism*; Elizabeth Abel, ed., *Writing and Sexual Difference* (Chicago: University of Chicago Press, 1982), and Newton and Rosenfelt, *Feminist Criticisms*. While further including in her discussion Carol Gilligan, *In a Different Voice: Psychological Theory and Women's Development* (Cambridge: Harvard University Press, 1982), and Virginia Woolf, *A Room of One's Own* (1929; reprint, London: Granada, 1977), her central focus is on Greene and Kahn, *Making a Difference*.
22 Gallop, *Around 1981*, 204.
23 Cora Kaplan, 'Pandora's Box: Subjectivity, Class, and Sexuality in Socialist Feminist Criticism,' in *Sea Changes*, 147–76; 148. Cited in Gallop, *Around 1981*, 196.
24 Gallop, *Around 1981*, 242.

25 The intertextual echoes continue. In the chapter mentioned earlier, entitled 'The Lure of the Mannish Lesbian', de Lauretis not only resumes Roof's focus on the concept of the lesbian as a 'lure of knowledge', but also engages in critical dialogue with the latter's theory of lesbian desire, as a 'desire for desire'. Cf. de Lauretis, *The Practice of Love*, 203–53.

26 Ibid., 149.

27 Ibid., 156; 155.

28 Ibid., 154.

29 Ibid., 157.

30 Ibid., 156.

31 I have explored the relations between identification and desire in more detail in 'Wat Weegt het Zwaarst: Freud en de Kwestie van het Primaat van Seksualiteit en Sekse' (What Comes First: Freud and the Question of the Primacy of Sexuality and Sex), *Krisis: Filosofisch Tijdschrift* XX (1994), 26–40.

32 Monique Wittig, 'The Straight Mind', in *The Straight Mind and Other Essays* (Boston: Beacon Press, 1992), 21–32; 32.

33 de Lauretis, *The Practice of Love*, 197; 198.

34 Deriving from the Latin verb *seducere*, to seduce literally means 'to lead away from proper conduct', to 'beguile' or 'win over' (*American Heritage Dictionary*).

35 Sigmund Freud, 'Femininity', in *New Introductory Lectures on Psychoanalysis*, ed. Angela Richards, tr. James Strachey, *Pelican Freud Library*, no. 2 (Harmondsworth: Penguin, 1988), 151–2.

36 Laplanche and Pontalis, *The Language of Psycho-Analysis*, 103. Since Freud continued to develop his ideas on 'defence' – as indeed on so many of his other concepts – throughout his career, numerous papers contain elaborations on the notion. Among the most important are S. Freud and J. Breuer, *Studies on Hysteria*, in *The Standard Edition of the Complete Psychological Works of Sigmund Freud*, tr. James Strachey, vol. XX (1895; reprint, London: The Hogarth Press, 1953–74); Sigmund Freud, *The Ego and the Mechanisms of Defence*, tr. Cecil Baines (1937; reprint, New York: International Universities Press, 1966); Sigmund Freud, *On Psychopathology: Inhibitions, Symptoms, and Anxiety*, in *The Pelican Freud Library*, ed. Angela Richards, tr. James Strachey, vol. 10 (1925; reprint, Harmondsworth: Penguin, 1987). By bringing together such scattered references, as well as through their in-depth discussions of psychoanalytic terms, Laplanche and Pontalis provide an indispensable source of knowledge and information, even for the more experienced reader of Freud. In my discussion of psychoanalytic concepts in the following paragraphs I will continue to rely on this volume.

37 Laplanche and Pontalis, *The Language of Psycho-analysis*, 105.

38 Cf. Sigmund Freud, 'The Unconscious', in *The Standard Edition of the Complete Psychological Works of Sigmund Freud*, tr. James Strachey, vol. XIV (London: The Hogarth Press, 1953–74); Sigmund Freud, 'Repression', in *The Standard Edition of the Complete Psychological*

Works of Sigmund Freud, tr. James Strachey, vol. XIV (London: The Hogarth Press, 1953–74).

39 Sigmund Freud, 'Fetishism', in *Sexuality and the Psychology of Love*, ed. Phillip Rieff, tr. Joan Rivière (New York: Collier Books/Macmillan Publishing Group, 1993), 205.

40 Laplanche and Pontalis, *The Language of Psycho-analysis*, 119.

41 Freud, 'Fetishism', 204.

42 Ibid., 206.

43 Ibid.

44 de Lauretis, *The Practice of Love*, 223.

45 See, e.g., Judith Butler, 'The Lesbian Phallus and the Morphological Imagination', *Differences: A Journal of Feminist Cultural Studies* 4, no. 1 (1992), 133–71; Elizabeth Grosz, 'Lesbian Fetishism?', *Differences: A Journal of Feminist Cultural Studies* 3, no. 2 (1991), 39–54. The 'model of "perverse" desire' developed by de Lauretis in *The Practice of Love* forms, to my mind, one of the most persuasive and enabling instances among such specifically lesbian acts of reappropriation.

46 Cf. Jacques Lacan, 'The Mirror Stage as Formative of the Function of the I as Revealed in Psychoanalytic Experience', in *Écrits: A Selection*, tr. Alan Sheridan (New York: Norton, 1977), 1–7.

47 See Jacques Lacan, *The Four Fundamental Concepts of Psycho-analysis*, tr. Alan Sheridan (New York: W.W. Norton, 1978).

48 Sigmund Freud, 'The Splitting of the Ego in the Defensive Process', in *Sexuality and the Psychology of Love*, ed. Phillip Rieff, tr. James Strachey (New York: Collier Books/Macmillan Publishing Group, 1993).

49 Freud, 'Fetishism', 206.

50 Ibid.

51 Butler, 'Imitation and Gender Insubordination', 20. See also chapter 2.

52 Sigmund Freud, 'Negation', in *The Standard Edition of the Complete Psychological Works of Sigmund Freud*, tr. James Strachey, vol. XIX (London: The Hogarth Press, 1953–74), 235–6.

53 See, for instance, Susan Faludi, *Backlash: The Undeclared War Against American Women* (New York: Anchor Books/Doubleday, 1991).

Epilogue

1 Shoshana Felman, *What Does a Woman Want? Reading and Sexual Difference* (Baltimore & London: The Johns Hopkins University Press, 1993), 118.

2 Mikhail M. Bakhtin, *Toward a Philosophy of the Act*, ed. Vadim Liapunov and Michael Holquist, tr. Vadim Liapunov (Austin: The University of Texas Press, 1993), 19.

3 Felman, *What Does a Woman Want?*, 127.

4 Bakhtin, *Toward a Philosophy of the Act*, 19.

5 Ibid.

Bibliography

Abbott, Sidney and Barbara Love, *Sappho Was a Right-on Woman: A Liberated View of Lesbianism.* 1972. Reprint. New York: Stein & Day, 1973.

Abel, Elizabeth, ed., *Writing and Sexual Difference.* Chicago: University of Chicago Press, 1982.

Abel, Elizabeth, Marianne Hirsch and Elizabeth Langland, eds, *The Voyage In: Fictions of Female Development.* Hanover & London: University Press of New England, 1983.

Abelove, Henry, Michèle Aina Barale and David M. Halperin, eds, *The Lesbian and Gay Studies Reader.* New York: Routledge, 1993.

Alexander, Paul, ed., *Ariel Ascending: Writings about Sylvia Plath.* New York: Harper & Row, 1984.

Althusser, Louis, 'Ideology and Ideological State Apparatuses (Notes towards an Investigation).' In *Essays on Ideology.* London: Verso, 1984. (1970)

Auerbach, Nina, *Communities of Women: An Idea in Fiction.* Cambridge: Harvard University Press, 1978.

Bakhtin, Mikhail M., *Towards a Philosophy of the Act.* Ed. Vadim Liapunov and Michael Holquist. Tr. Vadim Liapunov. Austin: University of Texas Press, 1993.

Bal, Mieke, *Narratologie: Essais sur la signification narrative dans quatre romans modernes.* Paris: Klinksieck, 1977.

Barrett, Michèle and Anne Phillips, eds, *Destabilizing Theory: Contemporary Feminist Debates.* Cambridge: Polity Press, 1992.

Benstock, Shari, 'Expatriate Sapphic Modernism: Entering Literary History.' In Karla Jay and Joanne Glasgow (eds), *Lesbian Texts and Contexts: Radical Revisions.* New York: New York University Press, 1990.

—— ed., *Feminist Issues in Literary Scholarship.* Bloomington: Indiana University Press, 1987.

—— *Women of the Left Bank: Paris, 1900–1940.* Austin: University of Texas Press, 1986.

Bernard-Douglas, Michael F., *Mikhail Bakhtin: Between Phenomenology and Marxism.* Cambridge: Cambridge University Press, 1994.

Boffin, Tessa and Jean Fraser, eds, *Stolen Glances: Lesbians Take Photographs.* London: Pandora, 1991.

Bowen, Elizabeth, *Friends and Relations.* 1931. Reprint. Harmondsworth: Penguin, 1982.

—— *The Heat of the Day.* 1949. Reprint. Harmondsworth: Penguin, 1983.

—— 'Notes on Writing a Novel.' In Spencer Curtis Brown (ed.), *Pictures and Conversations.* London: Allen Lane, 1975.

—— *Pictures and Conversations: Chapters of an Autobiography with Other Collected Writings.* Ed. Spencer Curtis Brown. London: Allen Lane, 1975.

—— 'Preface to *Stories by Elizabeth Bowen.*' In *Afterthought.* London: Longmans, 1962. (1957)

—— 'Preface to *The Last September.*' In *Afterthought.* London: Longmans, 1962. (1952)

Breines, Wini, *Young, White, and Miserable: Growing up Female in the Fifties.* Boston: Beacon Press, 1992.

Brodski, Bella and Celeste Schenck, eds, *Life/lines: Theorizing Women's Autobiography.* Ithaca: Cornell University Press, 1988.

Brooke, Jocelyn, *Elizabeth Bowen.* Supplement to *British Book News,* no. 28. London: Longmans, 1951.

Butler, Judith, *Bodies That Matter: On the Discursive Limits of 'Sex'.* New York: Routledge, 1994.

—— 'Imitation and Gender Insurbordination.' In Diana Fuss (ed.), *Inside/Out: Lesbian Theories, Gay Theories.* New York: Routledge, 1991.

—— 'The Lesbian Phallus and the Morphological Imagination.' *Differences: A Journal of Feminist Cultural Studies* 4, no. 1, 1992.

Butscher, Edward, ed., *Sylvia Plath: The Woman and the Work.* New York: Dodd, Mead & Co., 1977.

Cant, Bob and Susan Hemmings, eds, *Radical Records: Thirty Years of Lesbian Gay History.* London: Routledge, 1988.

Castle, Terry, *The Apparitional Lesbian: Female Homosexuality and Modern Culture.* New York: Columbia University Press, 1993.

Chauncey Jr, George, 'From Sexual Inversion to Homosexuality: Medicine and the Changing Conceptions of Female Deviance.' *Salmagundi* 68–9, Fall 1982/Winter 1983.

Clark, Katerina and Michael Holquist, *Mikhail Bakhtin.* Cambridge: Belknap Press of Harvard University, 1984.

Cohen, Barry M. et al., eds, *Multiple Personality Disorder from the Inside Out.* Baltimore: Sylvan Press, 1991.

Conn, Peter, *The Cambridge Illustrated History of American Literature.* London & New York: Guild Publishing, 1990.

Creed, Barbara, *The Monstrous-Feminine: Film, Feminism, Psychoanalysis.* London: Routledge, 1993.

Dalsimer, Katherine, *Female Adolescence: Psychoanalytic Reflections on Literature.* New Haven & London: Yale University Press, 1986.

Daly, Mary, *Gyn/Ecology: The Metaethics of Radical Feminism.* Boston: Beacon Press, 1978.

Doan, Laura, ed., *The Lesbian Postmodern*. New York: Columbia University Press, 1994.

Douglas, Susan J., *Where the Girls Are: Growing Up Female with the Mass Media*. 1994. Reprint. New York: Times Books/Random House, 1995.

Dubuy, Georges and Michelle Perrot, eds, *A History of Women in the West*, originally published as *Histoire des femmes en occident*, 1991–2. Reprint. Cambridge: Harvard University Press, 1992–5.

Ellis, Havelock, *Studies in the Psychology of Sex*. New York: Random House, 1936.

Erikson, Erik, *Identity: Youth and Crisis*. London: Faber & Faber, 1968.

Faderman, Lilian, ed., *Chloe plus Olivia: An Anthology of Lesbian Literature from the Seventeenth Century to the Present*. London: Penguin Books, 1994.

—— *Odd Girls and Twilight Lovers: A History of Lesbian Life in Twentieth-Century America*. New York: Columbia University Press, 1991.

—— *Surpassing the Love of Men: Romantic Friendship and Love Between Women from the Renaissance to the Present*. 1981. Reprint. London: Women's Press, 1985.

Faludi, Susan, *Backlash: The Undeclared War against American Women*. New York: Anchor Books/Doubleday, 1991.

Felman, Shoshana, *What Does a Woman Want? Reading and Sexual Difference*. Baltimore & London: Johns Hopkins University Press, 1993.

Forster, Jeanette H., *Sex Variant Women in Literature*. 1956. Reprint. Tallahassee: Naiad Press, 1985.

Foucault, Michel, 'Technologies of the Self.' In Luther H. Martin, Huck Gutman and Patrick H. Hutton (eds), *Technologies of the Self: A Seminar with Michel Foucault*. Amherst: University of Massachusetts Press, 1988.

Freud, Sigmund, *The Ego and the Mechanisms of Defence*. Tr. Cecil Baines. 1937. Reprint. New York: International Universities Press, 1966.

—— 'Femininity.' In Angela Richards (ed.), *New Introductory Lectures on Psychoanalysis*. Tr. James Strachey. Harmondsworth: Penguin, 1988.

—— 'Fetishism.' In Phillip Rieff (ed.), *Sexuality and the Psychology of Love*. Tr. Joan Rivière. New York: Collier Books/Macmillan Publishing Group, 1993. (1927)

—— 'Fragment of an Analysis of a Case of Hysteria.' In Angela Richards (ed.), *Case Histories I: 'Dora' and 'Little Hans'*. Tr. James Strachey. Harmondsworth: Penguin, 1977.

—— 'Negation.' In *The Standard Edition of the Complete Psychological Works of Sigmund Freud*. Tr. James Strachey. 24 vols. London: The Hogarth Press, 1953–74.

—— *On Psychopathology: Inhibitions, Symptoms, and Anxiety*. Ed. Angela Richards. Tr. James Strachey. 1925. Reprint. Harmondsworth: Penguin, 1987.

—— 'The Psychogenesis of a Case of Homosexuality in a Woman.' In Angela Richards (ed.), *Case Histories II: 'Rat Man', Schreber, 'Wolf Man', Female Homosexuality*. Tr. James Strachey. Harmondsworth: Penguin, 1987.

—— 'Repression.' In *The Standard Edition of the Complete Psychological*

Works of Sigmund Freud. Tr. James Strachey. 24 vols. London: The Hogarth Press, 1953–74.
—— 'Some Psychical Consequences of the Anatomical Distinction Between the Sexes.' In Phillip Rieff (ed.), *Sexuality and the Psychology of Love.* Tr. James Strachey. New York: Collier Books/Macmillan Publishing Group, 1993. (1925)
—— 'The Splitting of the Ego in the Defensive Process.' In Phillip Rieff (ed.), *Sexuality and the Psychology of Love.* Tr. James Strachey. New York: Collier Books/Macmillan Publishing Group, 1993. (1938)
—— 'The Unconscious.' In *The Standard Edition of the Complete Psychological Works of Sigmund Freud.* Tr. James Strachey. 24 vols. London: The Hogarth Press, 1953–74.
—— 'Wolf Man.' In Angela Richards (ed.), *Case Histories II: 'Rat Man', Schreber, 'Wolf Man', Female Homosexuality.* Tr. James Strachey. Harmondsworth: Penguin, 1987.
Freud, Sigmund and J. Breuer, *Studies on Hysteria.* In *The Standard Edition of the Complete Psychological Works of Sigmund Freud,* vol. XX. Tr. James Strachey. 1895. Reprint. London: The Hogarth Press, 1953–74.
Friedan, Betty, *The Feminine Mystique.* New York: Norton, 1963.
Frye, Marilyn, 'To Be and Be Seen: The Politics of Reality.' In *The Politics of Reality: Essays in Feminist Theory.* Trumansberg, NY: The Crossing Press, 1983.
Gallop, Jane, *Around 1981: Academic Feminist Literary Criticism.* London: Routledge, 1992.
—— *Feminism and Psychoanalysis: The Daughter's Seduction.* Ithaca and London: Cornell University Press and Macmillan, 1982.
Galvin, Angela, '*Basic Instinct*: Damning Dykes.' In Diane Hamer and Belinda Budge (eds), *The Good, the Bad, and the Gorgeous: Popular Culture's Romance with Lesbianism.* London: Pandora, 1994.
Genette, Gérard, *Narrative Discourse.* Tr. Jane Lewin. Oxford: Basil Blackwell, 1986.
Gever, Martha and Nathalie Magnan, 'The Same Difference: On Lesbian Representation.' In Tessa Boffin and Jean Fraser (eds), *Stolen Glances: Lesbians Take Photographs* London: Pandora, 1991. (1986)
Gibbs, Liz, ed., *Daring to Dissent: Lesbian Culture from Margin to Mainstream.* London: Cassell, 1994.
Gilligan, Carol, *In a Different Voice: Psychological Theory and Women's Development.* Cambridge: Harvard University Press, 1982.
Glendinning, Victoria, *Elizabeth Bowen: A Portrait of a Writer.* 1977. Reprint. Harmondsworth: Penguin, 1985.
Greene, Gayle and Coppélia Kahn, eds, *Making a Difference: Feminist Literary Criticism.* New York: Methuen, 1985.
Grier, Barbara, ed., *The Lesbian in Literature.* 3rd edn, Tallahassee: Naiad Press, 1981.
Griffin, Gabriele, *Heavenly Love: Lesbian Images in Twentieth-Century Women's Writing.* Manchester: Manchester University Press, 1993.
—— ed., *Outwrite: Lesbianism and Popular Culture.* London: Pluto Press, 1993.

Griggers, Camilla, 'Phantom and Reel Projections: Lesbians and the (Serial) Killing-Machine.' In Judith Halberstam and Ira Livingston (eds), *Posthuman Bodies*. Bloomington and Indianapolis: Indiana University Press, 1995.

Griggers, Cathy, 'Lesbian Bodies in the Age of (Post)Mechanical Reproduction.' In Laura Doan (ed.), *The Lesbian Postmodern*. New York: Columbia University Press, 1994.

Grosz, Elizabeth. 'Lesbian Fetishism?' *Differences: A Journal of Feminist Cultural Studies* 3, no. 2, 1991.

—— *Volatile Bodies: Toward a Corporeal Feminism*. Bloomington & Indianapolis: Indiana University Press, 1994.

Hamer, Diane and Belinda Budge, eds, *The Good, the Bad, and the Gorgeous: Popular Culture's Romance with Lesbianism*. London: Pandora, 1994.

Hart, Lynda, *Fatal Women: Lesbian Sexuality and the Mark of Aggression*. Princeton, NJ: Princeton University Press, 1994.

Hartsock, Nancy, 'Foucault on Power: A Theory for Women?' In Linda J. Nicholson (ed.), *Feminism/Postmodernism*. New York: Routledge, 1990.

Hayman, Ronald, *The Death and Life of Sylvia Plath*. London: Minerva, 1991.

Hekma, Gert, 'A History of Sexology: Social and Historical Aspects of Sexuality.' In Jan Bremmer (ed.), *From Sappho to de Sade: Moments in the History of Sexuality*. London: Routledge, 1989.

Hewitt, Douglas, *English Fiction of the Early Modern Period, 1890–1940*. London: Longmans, 1988.

hoogland, renée c., *Elizabeth Bowen: A Reputation in Writing*. New York: New York University Press, 1994.

—— 'From Marginality to Ex-Centricity: Feminist Critical Theory and the Case of Elizabeth Bowen.' Ph.D. diss. University of Amsterdam, 1991.

—— 'Perverted Knowledge: Lesbian Sexuality and Theory.' *Journal of Gender Studies* 3, no. 1, 1994.

—— 'Wat Weegt het Zwaarst: Freud en de Kwestie van het Primaat van Seksualiteit en Sekse' (What Comes First: Freud and the Question of the Primacy of Sexuality and Sex). *Krisis: Filosofisch Tijdschrift* XX, 1994.

hooks, bell, 'Homophobia in Black Communities.' In *Talking Back: Thinking Feminist, Thinking Black*. Boston: South End Press, 1989.

—— 'Writing the Subject: Reading *The Color Purple*.' In Henry Louis Gates Jr (ed.), *Reading Black, Reading Feminist: A Critical Anthology*. New York: Meridian, 1990.

Hutcheon, Linda, *A Poetics of Postmodernism: History, Theory, Fiction*. New York & London: Routledge, 1988.

Irigaray, Luce, 'Commodities among Themselves.' In *This Sex Which Is Not One*. Tr. Catherine Porter and Carolyn Burke. Ithaca: Cornell University Press, 1985. (1977)

Jagose, Annamarie, *Lesbian Utopics*. New York: Routledge, 1994.

Kaplan, Cora, 'Keeping the Color in *The Color Purple*.' In *Sea Changes: Culture and Feminism*. London: Verso, 1986.

——— 'Pandora's Box: Subjectivity, Class, and Sexuality in Socialist Feminist Criticism.' In *Sea Changes: Culture and Feminism.* London: Verso, 1986.

Katz, Jonathan, *Gay American History: Lesbians and Gay Men in the U.S.A.* 1976. Reprint. New York: Avon, 1978.

Keilson-Lauritz, Marita, 'Maske und Signal: Textstrategien der Homoerotik.' In Maria Kalveram and Wolfgang Popp (eds), *Homosexualitäten-Literarisch: Literaturwissenschaftliche Beiträge zum Internationalen Kongress 'Homosexuality which Homosexuality? Amsterdam 1987'.* Essen: Verlag Die Blaue Eule, 1991.

King, Katie, 'Audre Lorde's Lacquered Layerings: The Lesbian Bar as a Site of Literary Production.' In Sally Munt (ed.), *New Lesbian Criticism: Literary and Cultural Readings.* New York & London: Harvester Wheatsheaf, 1992.

Koedt, Anne, Ellen Levine and Anita Rapone, eds, *Radical Feminism.* New York: Quadrangle Books, 1973.

Kraakman, Dorelies, 'Vijf Maal Nul Is Nul.' In *Deugd en Ondeugd: Jaarboek voor Vrouwengeschiedenis.* Amsterdam: Stichting Beheer IISG, 1993.

Krafft-Ebing, Richard von, *Psychopathia Sexualis with Especial Reference to the Antipathic Sexual Instincts.* Tr. F. J. Rebman. 1886. Reprint. Brooklyn: Physicians and Surgeons Books Co., 1908.

Kristeva, Julia, 'The Adolescent Novel.' In John Fletcher and Andrew Benjamin (eds), *Abjection, Melancholia, and Love: The Work of Julia Kristeva.* London & New York: Routledge, 1990.

——— 'Motherhood According to Bellini.' In Léon Roudiez (ed.), *Desire in Language: A Semiotic Approach to Literature and Art.* Tr. Alice Jardine, Thomas Gora and Léon Roudiez. Oxford: Blackwell, 1980.

Lacan, Jacques, *The Four Fundamental Concepts of Psycho-analysis.* Tr. Alan Sheridan. New York: W.W. Norton, 1978.

——— 'The Mirror Stage as Formative of the Function of the I as Revealed in Psychoanalytic Experience.' In *Écrits: A Selection.* Tr. Alan Sheridan. New York: Norton, 1977.

Lane, Gary, ed., *Sylvia Plath: New Views on the Poetry.* Baltimore: Johns Hopkins Press, 1979.

——— and Maria Stevens, *Sylvia Plath: A Bibliography.* Metuchen, NJ: Scarecrow, 1978.

Laplanche, Jean and Jean-Bertrand Pontalis, *The Language of Psycho-analysis.* Tr. Donald Nicholson-Smith. 1967. Reprint. London: Karnac Books and the Institute of Psycho-Analysis, 1988.

Lassner, Phyllis, *Elizabeth Bowen.* London: Macmillan Education, 1990.

de Lauretis, Teresa, 'Desire in Narrative.' In *Alice Doesn't: Feminism, Semiotics, Cinema.* Bloomington: Indiana University Press, 1988.

——— ed., *Feminist Studies/Critical Studies.* Bloomington: Indiana University Press, 1986.

——— 'Perverse Desire: The Lure of the Mannish Lesbian.' *Australian Feminist Studies* 13, 1991.

——— *The Practice of Love: Lesbian Sexuality and Perverse Desire.* Bloomington & Indianapolis: Indiana University Press, 1994.

—— 'Queer Theory: Lesbian and Gay Sexualities, An Introduction.' *Differences: A Journal of Feminist Cultural Studies* 5, no. 2, 1991.

—— 'Sexual Indifference and Lesbian Representation.' *Theatre Journal* 5, 1988.

—— 'The Technology of Gender.' In *Technologies of Gender: Essays on Theory, Film, and Fiction.* Bloomington & Indianapolis: Indiana University Press, 1987.

Lee, Hermione, *Elizabeth Bowen: An Estimation.* London & Totowa: Vision/Barnes and Noble, 1981.

Light, Alison, 'Fear of the Happy Ending: *The Color Purple*, Reading and Racism.' In Linda Anderson (ed.), *Plotting Change: Contemporary Women's Fiction.* London, Melbourne, Auckland: Edward Arnold, 1990.

MacPherson, Pat, *Reflecting on The Bell Jar.* London & New York: Routledge, 1991.

Marcus, Jane, 'Still Practice: A/Wrested Alphabet.' In Shari Benstock (ed.), *Feminist Issues in Literary Scholarship.* Bloomington: Indiana University Press, 1987.

Marks, Elaine, 'Lesbian Intertextuality.' In Elaine Marks and George Stambolian (eds), *Homosexualities and French Literature*, Ithaca: Cornell University Press, 1979.

Martin, Elaine, 'Mothers, Madness, and the Middle Class in *The Bell Jar* and *Les Mots pour le Dire.*' *French-American Review* 5, Spring 1981.

Martin, Wallace, *Recent Theories of Narrative.* Ithaca & London: Cornell University Press, 1986.

Meijer, Maaike, *De Lust tot Lezen: Nederlandse Dichteressen en het Literaire Systeem.* Amsterdam: Sara/van Gennep, 1988.

Merleau-Ponty, Maurice, *The Prose of the World.* Ed. Claude Lefort. Tr. John O'Neill. 1969. Reprint. Evanston: Northwestern University Press, 1973.

Miles, Rosalind, *The Female Form: Women Writers and the Conquest of the Novel.* London: Routledge, 1990.

Moers, Ellen, *Literary Women.* 1963. Reprint. London: Women's Press, 1978.

Munt, Sally, '*Somewhere Over the Rainbow* ... Postmodernism and the Fiction of Sarah Schulman.' In Sally Munt (ed.), *New Lesbian Criticism: Literary and Cultural Readings.* New York & London: Harvester Wheatsheaf, 1992.

—— ed., *New Lesbian Criticism: Literary and Cultural Readings.* Hemel Hempstead: Harvester Wheatsheaf, 1992.

Myron, Nancy and Charlotte Bunch, eds, *Lesbianism and the Women's Movement.* Baltimore: Diana Press, 1975.

Newton, Esther, *Mother's Camp: Female Impersonators in America.* Chicago: University of Chicago Press, 1972.

—— 'The Mythic Mannish Lesbian: Radclyffe Hall and the New Woman.' In Martin Bauml Duberman, Martha Vicinus and George Chauncey Jr (eds), *Hidden from History: Reclaiming the Gay and Lesbian Past.* New York: New American Library, 1987.

Newton, Judith and Deborah Rosenfelt, eds, *Feminist Criticisms and Social Change: Sex, Race and Class in Literature and Culture.* New York: Methuen, 1985.
Pattynama, Pamela, 'De Herinnering aan het Oude Verhaal' (Old Stories Remembered). *Lover* 2, 1989.
—— 'Maskering en Geheimhouding' (Disguise and Secrecy). In Margriet Prinssen and Lucie Th. Vermeij (eds), *Schrijfsters in der Jaren Vijftig.* Amsterdam: An Dekker, 1990.
—— *Passages: Vrouwelijke Adolescentie als Verhaal en Vertoog.* Kampen: Kok Agora, 1992.
Plath, Sylvia, *The Bell Jar.* 1963. Reprint. London: Faber & Faber, 1980.
—— *The Journals of Sylvia Plath.* New York: Ballantine, 1983.
—— *Letters Home: Correspondence 1950–1963.* New York: Harper & Row, 1975.
Pratt, Annis, *Archetypal Patterns in Women's Fiction.* Brighton: Harvester, 1981.
Putnam, Frank W., *Diagnosis & Treatment of Multiple Personality Disorder.* New York & London: The Guilford press, 1989.
Radicalesbians. 'The Woman-Identified Woman.' In Anita Rapone et al. (eds), *Radical Feminism.* New York: Quadrangle Books, 1973.
Raiskin, Judith, 'Inverts and Hybrids: Lesbian Rewritings of Sexual and Racial Identities.' In Laura Doan (ed.), *The Lesbian Postmodern.* New York: Columbia University Press, 1994.
Rich, Adrienne, 'Compulsory Heterosexuality and Lesbian Existence.' In Ann Snitow et al. (eds), *Desire: The Politics of Sexuality.* London: Virago, 1984. (1981)
Rimmon-Kenan, Shlomith, *Narrative Fiction: Contemporary Poetics.* London: Methuen, 1983.
Rogers, Robert, *A Psychoanalytic Study of the Double in Literature.* Detroit: Wayne State University Press, 1970.
Roof, Judith, *A Lure of Knowledge: Lesbian Sexuality and Theory.* New York: Columbia University Press, 1991.
Rose, Jacqueline, *The Haunting of Sylvia Plath.* London: Verso, 1991.
Rubin Gayle, 'Thinking Sex: Notes for a Radical Theory of Sexuality.' In Henry Abelove et al. (eds), *The Lesbian and Gay Studies Reader.* New York: Routledge, 1993.
—— 'The Traffic in Women: Notes Toward a Political Economy of Sex.' In Reina Rayter (ed.), *Toward an Anthropology of Women.* New York: Monthly Review Press, 1975.
Rule, Jane, *Lesbian Images.* Freedom, Calif.: The Crossing Press, 1975.
Seidman, Steven, *Romantic Longings: Love in America, 1830–1980.* New York & London: Routledge, 1991.
Showalter, Elaine, *A Literature of Their Own: British Women Novelists from Brontë to Lessing.* 1977. Reprint. London: Virago, 1978.
—— ed., *The New Feminist Criticism: Essays on Women, Literature, Theory.* New York: Pantheon, 1985.
Silverman, Kaja, *The Acoustic Mirror: The Female Voice in Psychoanalysis and Cinema.* Bloomington & Indianapolis: Routledge, 1988.

Smelik, Anneke, 'What Meets the Eye: Feminist Film Studies.' In Rosemarie Buikema and Anneke Smelik (eds), *Women's Studies and Culture: A Feminist Introduction.* London & New Jersey: Zed Books, 1995.

Smith, Barbara, 'Toward a Black Feminist Criticism.' In Elaine Showalter (ed.), *The New Feminist Criticism: Essays on Women, Literature, and Theory.* New York: Pantheon Books, 1985. (1977)

Smith-Rosenberg, Caroll, 'The Female World of Love and Ritual.' In *Disorderly Conduct: Visions of Gender in Victorian America.* New York: Oxford University Press, 1985.

—— 'The New Woman as Androgyne: Social Disorder and Gender Crisis 1870–1936.' In *Disorderly Conduct: Visions of Gender in Victorian America.* New York: Oxford University Press, 1985.

Sniader-Lanser, Susan, *The Narrative Act: Point of View in Prose Fiction.* Princeton: Princeton University Press, 1981.

Snitow, Ann, Christine Stansell and Sharon Thomas, eds, *Powers of Desire: The Politics of Sexuality.* 1983. Reprint. London: Virago, 1984.

Spivak, Gayatri Chakravorty, 'Explanation and Culture: Marginalia.' In *In Other Worlds: Essays in Cultural Politics.* Routledge: New York, 1988.

—— 'French Feminism in an International Frame.' In *In Other Worlds: Essays in Cultural Politics.* New York: Routledge, 1988.

Stanton, Domna C., Introduction to *Discourses of Sexuality: From Aristotle to AIDS.* Ann Arbor: University of Michigan Press, 1992.

Stein, Arlene, ed., *Sisters, Sexperts, Queens: Beyond the Lesbian Nation.* New York: Plume, 1993.

Stevenson, Anne, *Bitter Fame: A Life of Sylvia Plath.* Boston: Houghton Mifflin, 1989.

Stimpson, Catherine, 'Afterword: Lesbian Studies in the 1990s.' In Karla Jay and Joanne Glasgow (eds), *Lesbian Texts and Contexts: Radical Revisions.* New York: New York University Press, 1990.

—— 'Zero Degree Deviancy: The Lesbian Novel in English.' *Critical Inquiry* 8, 1981.

Tabor, Stephen, *Sylvia Plath: An Analytic Bibliography.* London & New York: Mansell Publishing, 1986.

Verschoyle, Derek, *The English Novelists: A Survey of the Novel by Twenty Contemporary Novelists.* London: Chatto and Windus, 1936.

Wagner, Linda W., ed., *Critical Essays on Sylvia Plath.* Boston: G. K. Hall, 1984.

—— 'Plath's *The Bell Jar* as Female Bildungsroman.' *Women's Studies* 12, 1983.

Wagner-Martin, Linda, *The Bell Jar: A Novel of the Fifties.* New York: Twayne, 1992.

—— *Sylvia Plath: A Biography.* London and New York: Simon & Schuster, 1987.

Walker, Alice, *The Color Purple.* London: Women's Press, 1992.

Weiss, Andrea, *Vampires and Violets: Lesbians in Film.* 1992. Reprint. New York: Penguin, 1993.

White, Barbara, *Growing Up Female: Adolescent Girlhood in American Fiction.* Connecticut & London: Greenwood Press, 1985.

Wiesen Cook, Blanche, 'The Historical Denial of Lesbianism.' *Radical History Review* 20, 1979.
—— '"Women Alone Stir My Imagination"': Lesbianism and the Cultural Tradition.' In Wayne W. Dynes and Stephen Donaldson (eds), *Studies in Homosexuality: Lesbianism*. New York: Garland Publishing, 1992.
Wittig, Monique, 'Homo Sum.' In *The Straight Mind and Other Essays*. Boston: Beacon Press, 1992. (1990)
—— 'On the Social Contract.' In *The Straight Mind and Other Essays*. Boston: Beacon Press, 1992. (1989)
—— 'One Is Not Born a Woman.' In *The Straight Mind and Other Essays*. Boston: Beacon Press, 1992. (1981)
—— 'The Straight Mind.' In *The Straight Mind and Other Essays*. Boston: Beacon Press, 1992. (1980)
—— *The Straight Mind and Other Essays*. Boston: Beacon Press, 1992.
Wittig, Monique and Sande Zeig, *Lesbian Peoples: Material for a Dictionary*. New York: Avon, 1979.
Woolf, Virginia, *A Room of One's Own*. 1929. Reprint. London: Granada, 1977.
Zimmerman, Bonnie, 'Exiting from Patriarchy: The Lesbian Novel of Development.' In Marianne Hirsch and Elizabeth Langland (eds), *The Voyage In: Fictions of Female Development*. Hanover & London: The University Press of New England, 1985.
—— *The Safe Sea of Women: Lesbian Fiction 1969–1989*. Boston: Beacon Press, 1990.
—— 'What Has Never Been: An Overview of Lesbian Feminist Criticism.' In Gayle Greene and Coppelía Kahn (eds), *Making a Difference: Feminist Literary Criticism*. London: Methuen, 1985.

Index

BETWEEN MEN ~ BETWEEN WOMEN
LESBIAN AND GAY STUDIES

LILLIAN FADERMAN AND LARRY GROSS, EDITORS

Edward Alwood, *Straight News: Gays, Lesbians, and the News Media*
Corinne E. Blackmer and Patricia Juliana Smith, editors, *En Travesti:
Women, Gender Subversion, Opera*
Alan Bray, *Homosexuality in Renaissance England*
Joseph Bristow, *Effeminate England: Homoerotic Writing After 1885*
Beverly Burch, *Other Women: Lesbian Experience and Psychoanalytic Theory
of Women*
Claudia Card, *Lesbian Choices*
Joseph Carrier, *De Los Otros: Intimacy and Homosexuality Among Mexican Men*
John Clum, *Acting Gay: Male Homosexuality in Modern Drama*
Gary David Comstock, *Violence Against Lesbians and Gay Men*
Laura Doan, editor, *The Lesbian Postmodern*
Allen Ellenzweig, *The Homoerotic Photograph: Male Images
from Durieu/Delacroix to Mapplethorpe*
Lillian Faderman, *Odd Girls and Twilight Lovers: A History of Lesbian Life in
Twentieth-Century America*
Linda D. Garnets and Douglas C. Kimmel, editors, *Psychological Perspectives on
Lesbian and Gay Male Experiences*
Richard D. Mohr, *Gays/Justice: A Study of Ethics, Society, and Law*
Sally Munt, editor, *New Lesbian Criticism: Literary and Cultural Readings*
Timothy F. Murphy and Suzanne Poirier, editors, *Writing AIDS:
Gay Literature, Language, and Analysis*
Noreen O'Connor and Joanna Ryan, *Wild Desires and Mistaken Identities:
Lesbianism and Psychoanalysis*
Don Paulson with Roger Simpson, *An Evening in the Garden of Allah:
A Gay Cabaret in Seattle*
Judith Roof, *Come As You Are: Sexuality and Narrative*
Judith Roof, *A Lure of Knowledge: Lesbian Sexuality and Theory*
Claudia Schoppmann, *Days of Masquerade: Life Stories of Lesbians
During the Third Reich*
Alan Sinfield, *The Wilde Century: Effeminacy, Oscar Wilde, and the Queer Moment*
Jane McIntosh Snyder, *Lesbian Desire in the Lyrics of Sappho*
Chris Straayer: *Deviant Eyes, Deviant Bodies: Sexual Re-Orientations
in Film and Video*
Thomas Waugh, *Hard to Imagine: Gay Male Eroticism in Photography and Film
from Their Beginnings to Stonewall*
Kath Weston, *Families We Choose: Lesbians, Gays, Kinship*
Kath Weston, *Render me, Gender Me: Lesbians Talk Sex, Class, Color, Nation,
Studmuffins . . .*
Carter Wilson, *Hidden in the Blood: A Personal Investigation of AIDS in the Yucatán*